Instead of seeing the rug pulled from under us, we can learn to dance on a shifting carpet.

Thomas Crum

This book is dedicated to my dear friend Kathy Pontifex who is no longer here to share the dance of life with me.

Acknowledgements

Many thanks to Lucas House for his insightful and artful cartoons. Thanks also to Alex Schiller who was with me when this book was just an idea and who strongly encouraged me to develop it further and contributed useful ideas on the structure. Thanks must go as well to all my clients and colleagues who have informed the writing of this book. Particular thanks to Kathryn McEwen, a colleague and friend with whom I have collaborated on many of the topics over the years.

Learn to Dance on a Moving Carpet

How to create a balanced
and meaningful life

A 'go to' guide for adapting
to modern day pressure and problems

Jacky Dakin

First published 2015 by:
Australian Academic Press Group Pty. Ltd.
18 Victor Russell Drive
Samford Valley QLD 4520, Australia
www.australianacademicpress.com.au

Copyright © 2015 Jacky Dakin

Copying for educational purposes
The *Australian Copyright Act 1968* (Cwlth) allows a maximum of one chapter or 10% of this book, whichever is the greater, to be reproduced and/or communicated by any educational institution for its educational purposes provided that the educational institution (or the body that administers it) has given a remuneration notice to Copyright Agency Limited (CAL) under the Act.
For details of the CAL licence for educational institutions contact:
Copyright Agency Limited, 19/157 Liverpool Street, Sydney, NSW 2000.
E-mail info@copyright.com.au

Production and communication for other purposes
Except as permitted under the Act, for example a fair dealing for the purposes of study, research, criticism or review, no part of this book may be reproduced, stored in a retrieval system, or transmitted in any form or by any means electronic, mechanical, photocopying, recording or otherwise without prior written permission of the copyright holder.

Learn to Dance on a Moving Carpet: Creating a Balanced and Meaningful Life

ISBN   9781922117427 (paperback)
ISBN   9781922117434 (ebook)

Publisher & Copy Editor: Stephen May

Illustrator: Lucas House

Cover design: Maria Biaggini, The Letter Tree

Page design & typesetting: Australian Academic Press

Printing: Lightning Source

Contents

About the Author vi

Preface vii

Chapter 1. Self Awareness: The Key to a Better Life
How to know yourself better 1

Chapter 2. Fortify Your Physical and Mental Fitness
How to keep your mind and body strong and healthy 9

Chapter 3. Sleep Soundly
How to get a good night's sleep 19

Chapter 4. Throw Away Negative Thoughts
How to think more positively 27

Chapter 5. Stay Stress Savvy
How to better manage life's stressors 35

Chapter 6. Become Fearless
How to cope with anxiety 47

Chapter 7. Rise Above the Dark Clouds
How to survive despite depression 57

Chapter 8. When the Going Gets Tough…
How to build resilience to beat stress 69

Chapter 9. Confidence is Cool
How to develop confidence and manage emotions 81

Chapter 10. Raise the Bar on Relationships
How to get on better with people in life and work 91

Chapter 11. Come Back from Setbacks
How to survive when things go wrong 101

Chapter 12. Seize the Day!
How to live life to the full 109

Chapter 13. Dance towards Your Dreams
How to create the life you want 121

Personal Action Planner 131

Bibliography 133

About the Author

Jacky Dakin is an experienced psychologist, organisational development consultant, facilitator and executive coach. She is a regular guest presenter and keynote speaker at seminars and conferences, runs her own organisational consulting business, coupled with a private practice in clinical and counselling psychology. She is also a principal of a coaching consortium with professional colleagues.

She has a passion for helping people be the best they can whether personally or professionally. One of her greatest joys is when she sees her clients turn a corner and start overcoming their own particular obstacles. They can then make the positive changes which move them closer towards their own definition of success.

Jacky is active on several boards and committees, regularly mentors younger colleagues and students, and volunteers for various organisations. She has co-authored a successful book 'Short Poppies Can Grow: Confidence at Work' and a recently published e-book 'How to be successful despite yourself: Don't Kill Your Hamster'. She was formerly a regular co-columnist in the South Australian Advertiser, Saturday Review.

Jacky is a past finalist in the Telstra Business Woman of the Year and is a registered Marriage Celebrant.

Preface

In the normal course of my work I see many people who feel they have lost their way and are struggling with different aspects of their lives. Often my clients feel they are facing insurmountable hurdles to achieving wellbeing and a sense of fulfilment in their lives. Interestingly, sometimes their problems can be readily addressed with a short intervention and providing relevant education on the issue at hand.

With this in mind, I decided to package up some of the key concepts and actions I believe will help in coping with modern day pressures and problems and present it in a comprehensive and accessible self-help guide. This book includes ideas and strategies based on more than 25 years of experience, combined with latest research.

From feedback sought from a range of counselling and coaching clients, there appeared to be a need for this concise and reader-friendly book. It will 'kick start' readers towards taking action to achieve balance in their lives and to build the resilience required to enable them to adapt to the constant pressures and changes that occur in today's world. Doing so will help them derive greater meaning and purpose on a day-to-day basis, which in turn will lead to a happier and more fulfilling existence.

'Learn to dance on a moving carpet' is an analogy for the need to find balance in a fast paced and rapidly changing world. This book is a quick 'go to' guide for dealing with many common challenges in modern life. Understanding these will help readers to refocus their attention and stand stronger in a moving world.

I have adopted the premise that life is like a moving carpet and used dance as a metaphor for the journey through life. We need to be able to stand steady despite the shifts and shakes in its rhythm. If we become more self-aware, flexible and open to new experiences, we will more readily learn what often turn out to be quite simple strategies to cope with life's unexpected twists and turns. As a result we are more likely to find meaning in what we do and create for ourselves greater strength and ability to live our lives. We will also develop a greater feeling of wellbeing and may even discover a sense of happiness.

The chapters in this book provide the foundations for positive change and the exercises included will help those who wish to embrace these ideas. Experience has demonstrated that making some small changes in the areas covered can have a huge impact on overall wellbeing. Sometimes there can be a 'snowball effect' resulting in a virtual avalanche of positive effects over time.

Revisiting the concepts and strategies presented in this book from time to time will help to continue lifelong growth.

Jacky Dakin
December 2014

Chapter 1

Self-awareness: The Key to a Better Life

How to know yourself better

Dance Step: The Waltz

This dance evokes many emotions — from sadness to happiness to joy. The intimate circular motion provides new ways of how people relate to each other and to society as a whole.

To really know yourself is to be self-aware. To be self-aware means that you understand your own individuality and that you have a realistic perception of your own personality and your strengths and weaknesses. If you truly know yourself, you will be conscious of your motives, needs and fears. You will be aware of your deeper feelings, dreams and desires.

The more you understand who you are and live your life with awareness, the better you will be able to accept or change yourself when this is needed. Being willing and knowing how to make positive changes within yourself will in turn allow you to change the way you interact with others.

To have greater self-awareness or understanding means to have a better grasp of reality.
Dalai Lama

To enhance self-awareness, develop your communication skills. Effective communication will help you to build stronger relationships with people at both a personal and professional level so you can receive and act on feedback from others. This will allow you to more easily overcome any conflict or differences that may arise.

Responsibility and possibility through awareness

With self-awareness comes a sense of responsibility. This includes personal responsibility to live a healthy and happy life and to give and take in equal measures; responsibility to contribute and take an active part in life; responsibility to be genuinely interested in and compassionate towards those around us; responsibility to stay mindful that we also need to develop awareness of our inner life.

If you take this approach, you will be better able to see new possibilities for yourself and the relationships in your life.

Self-awareness gives you the power to make these possibilities happen. It will help you to find the right career, the right partner, the right friends and the right pathway in life. It will help you stay physically and mentally stronger.

Being able to see the many possibilities that surround you allows you to take advantage of them. They are endless but are easy to overlook if you are not seeing life clearly or are unaware they exist. If you strive to reach these possibilities you are likely to be rewarded by meaningful relationships and captivating and challenging experiences. No matter what the outcome, you will be richer for the journey.

Self awareness will not change you dramatically overnight but every time you bring new awareness to your life you will change in some small way. Being self-aware will allow you to create a contented and fulfilled life and in many instances to find peace within yourself.

I think the key to transforming your life is to be aware of who you are.

Deepak Chopra

BALANCE ACTION STEPS

How well do you know yourself? A self-awareness quiz.

Try this simple quiz now and answer as many of the questions as you can. Try it again after reading the book and see if the answers come to you more easily. If you still can't answer all the questions, ask someone who knows you well to help out.

1. What type of people do I enjoy spending time with and why?
2. When do I feel the most angry or frustrated?
   What is it about those situations that cause me to feel that way?
3. Am I currently doing the type of work I love to do?
   If not, what type of work would I like to do?

4. What skills have I acquired that I'm proud of?
5. What accomplishments am I proud of?
6. What are five of my greatest strengths?
7. List three situations or times when you felt the happiest in your life. What do you think caused you to feel that way?

Two great tips for creating greater self-awareness

1. Try taking an awareness break each day

Awareness breaks are very simple and yet can be very powerful. They require you to stop whatever is occurring at the moment for around half a minute and pay close attention. Then you notice what is happening to you and around you. You can choose a new way of 'being and doing' in that moment.

If you are usually quite inner focused but not so connected to what is going on externally, use your awareness breaks to notice what is happening around you and what is going on out there in the world.

If you are someone who is very present and tend not to look inward very often, try some internal reflection with your awareness breaks. Notice your thoughts, your feelings and your current state of being. Some people even have a visual experience of what is going on inside them.

> **Balance Action Steps**
>
> Why not try an awareness break right now?
>
> Just stop what you are doing, thinking, saying or being for 30 seconds and focus closely, both internally and externally. Really notice what is happening to you and around you. As well, notice how you feel.

2. Practise mindfulness in your life

Mindfulness is about being fully aware of what we are doing at any given time. We tend to do many things purely out of habit such as eating or getting ready in the mornings for example. Being mindful is about slowing down our thoughts and actions and really focusing on what we are doing so that it comes fully into awareness.

Practicing a mindful approach can help relieve stress and anxiety. Mindfulness meditation is now being used frequently by medical and psychological therapists to support and enhance their usual practice. It is being used in the treatment of depression, anxiety and chronic pain, as well as addictions and other psychological disorders. Recent research has also shown that people who regularly practise mindfulness have improved immune functioning.

When applying mindfulness to a particular situation, we generally relax our bodies, slow down our breathing and focus on the situation. These acts in themselves are doing something different as we are creating more awareness. This then helps us to have a variety of thoughts and experiences and to just let them happen without reacting to them.

High levels of awareness enhance all life activities. Pleasant experiences become more so as mindfulness allows us to be more fully 'in the moment'. As well, experiences that are normally mundane and even boring, such as washing dishes or the car, can become more interesting and of a better quality experience as you focus mindfully on them. Even those people who believe that exercise is a 'necessary evil' report that by using mindfulness, it can become easier and more interesting.

Balance Action Steps

Try going for a mindful walk either now or very soon. Here's how to do it.

- Take a walk in a pleasant surrounding and focus your awareness on your breathing as you walk. Keep returning to this focus from time to time.
- Allow yourself to become aware of any sights, sounds, smells or physical sensations that may be present. Focus your awareness briefly on these and then return to being mindful of your breathing.
- If persistent distracting thoughts come up, simply notice them, and return your awareness to your breathing.

When you return, write down what you experienced during the mindful walk. Then, reflect on the following questions:

- What thoughts, memories, associations or distracting thoughts came up during the walk?
- What sights, sounds or smells did you notice during the walk?
- What external physical sensations did you notice?
- What internal feelings came up during the walk?

Use Self-awareness to get the most out of this book

You will notice that following the last chapter (Chapter 13) there is a page headed *Personal Action Planner.* This has each chapter listed with an accompanying space.

At the end of each chapter write down on this page something that you feel you would like to change or do differently. List the one idea from each chapter that has had the most impact on you. Of course you can list more than one if you like.

This summary of the things that were most important or resonated with you the most in each chapter will help you organise your thoughts and take action. It will also stop you feeling overwhelmed. You don't need to completely overhaul your life but you are likely to benefit from making some useful changes.

At the end of the book you will have a list of 13 actions that you can take or 13 ways that you can use to make your life more positive. This will go side by side with the last chapter 'Dance Towards Your Dreams' by helping you to begin turning those dreams into reality.

> *When you are looking in the mirror, you are looking at the problem. But, remember, you are also looking at the solution.*
>
> **Anonymous**

Replay

- Self-awareness is getting to know yourself.
- Being self-aware allows you to accept or change who you are.
- Develop self-awareness to see new possibilities in life.
- Taking personal responsibility brings rewards.
- Use Awareness Breaks and Mindfulness to enhance self-awareness.
- Use Self-awareness to get the most out of this book.

Remember to pick one action from this chapter to include in the Personal Action Planner at the end of the book.

Learn to Dance on a Moving Carpet: Creating a balanced and meaningful life

Chapter 2

Fortify Your Physical and Mental Fitness

How to keep your mind and body strong and healthy

Dance Step: Tap

This vigorous and energetic dance is like creating music with your feet and dancing to it at the same time. The dancers are considered to be musicians.

Just as physical fitness is important for good health, energy and longevity, so is staying mentally fit. Both physical and mental fitness contribute to maintaining a strong and healthy immune system. They are the body's defense system against disease and keep us well and alive.

We all know that a good balanced diet and regular exercise are essential for physical fitness. You need to invest in your body what you expect it to return to you on a daily basis so as to build physical resilience and wellbeing.

Your mind is just like your body. If you exercise it properly and look after it, you can expect to stay mentally well and get a lot more out of life. It is important to allow yourself to take regular breaks from the pressures of life. On a daily basis focusing for even a short time on mental fitness strategies will provide immediate positive benefits and build mental resilience. You will feel more alert and alive and have the energy to do what is required of you and what you want to do.

> *Remember, you live within the mind, body and environment created by your choices.*
> **Dr Hal, Life and Mental Fitness Coach**

The 'Five Habits for Physical and Mental Fitness' are critical factors for staying physically well and creating mental resilience (See below).

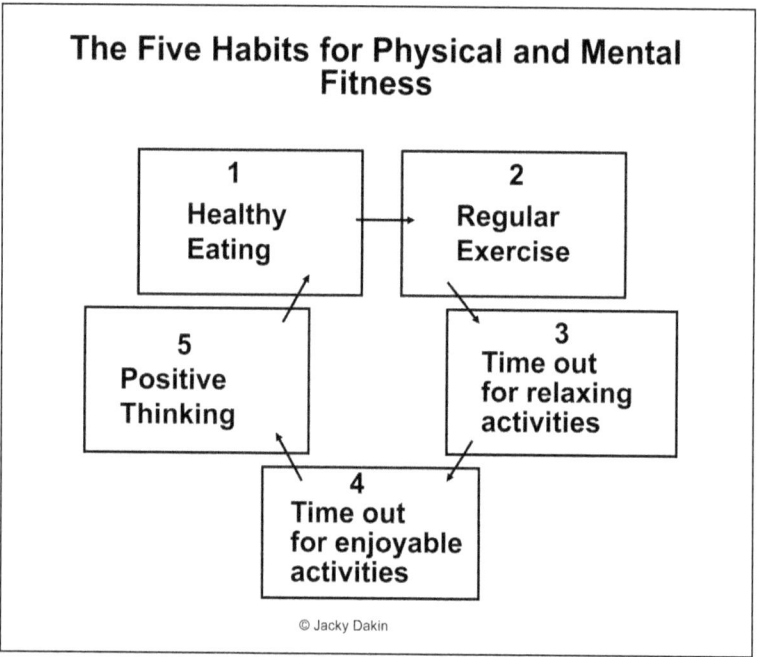

Habit 1 — Healthy Eating

We all know the saying 'We are what we eat'. Research shows that there is a range of benefits for healthy eaters. Some of these include a better attention span, more energy and a stronger ability to ward off sickness.

It is important to eat healthy, regular meals with plenty of vegetables and fruit. When we are stressed we may tend to overeat so we need to carefully manage portion size. A good tip is to use a smaller plate so it looks like you are eating more. It is useful to avoid excess carbohydrates and fats and to cut down caffeine, alcohol and nicotine.

Sometimes time pressures or mental health issues cause people to skip meals, which is equally bad for the body. If you don't put enough fuel in your car what happens? It stops running. And so will your body without sufficient nutrition.

Balance Action Steps

Stop for a moment and consider the following:

- Are you eating three healthy meals per day?
- Is your food intake balanced?
- Do you drink too much coffee (more than 2–3 cups per day)?
- Do you drink too much alcohol? Too much is if you are:
    - A woman who has more than 3 drinks every day or 21 drinks per week.
    - A man who has more than 5 drinks every day or 35 drinks per week.
- Do you smoke?
- What positive changes can you make?

Habit 2 — Regular Exercise

It is well known that regular physical activity improves physical and psychological wellbeing and can reduce depression and anxiety. Exercise is active relaxation and a great tension reliever, however you really need to exercise for 30 to 40 minutes three times a week to gain the benefits of stress relief. (For gaining fitness and losing weight, the experts recommend daily exercise).

You don't have to join a gym, although becoming part of an exercise group or a gym can also reduce isolation. You will meet new people with the same interest or a common goal of becoming fitter and healthier. Of course you need to be sufficiently motivated to actually go.

If the thought of joining a gym is a real turn off for you, walking is an excellent method of exercise and stress relief. It can also be a good social activity to catch up with friends at the same time. A fun way to reward yourself after a good long walk with your pals is to finish up with a visit to a local café, although make sure you limit the croissants or chocolate cake!

Whatever form your physical activity takes, it is good to find an 'exercise buddy' as this will help to motivate you to keep at it. You may find that you will push yourself more to do the walk or go to the gym so as not to let your buddy down. It will also help if you make the activity a regular part of your daily or weekly routine and even use a diary to record your progress.

Balance Action Steps

Ask yourself honestly:

- Are you are doing enough exercise on a weekly basis?
- Do you have an exercise buddy?

- Is it part of your normal routine?
- What can you do better or more of?

Habit 3 — Time Out for Relaxing Activities

While active relaxation is great for tension relief, it is passive relaxation that actually counteracts the stress response by slowing us down mentally and physically.

To create wellbeing it is necessary from time to time to 'switch off', yet often people don't make the time or even try to do this — or they dismiss the possibility by saying they are unable to do it. Many of us are sadly lacking in 'Me Time', yet this is critical to achieve appropriate work/life balance.

So what can you do? Try meditation, relaxation tapes, yoga or massage. In addition, gardening, a slow walk, pleasant reading and a variety of crafts can all be appropriately relaxing activities.

Alternatively, listen to gentle music, have a spa, bath, or shower to wind down. A good aid to relaxation is to use aromatherapy. Lavender oil for example aids relaxation and is widely used in hospices and birthing units.

Balance Action Steps

Consider what you can introduce into your life to help and write down some actions you can do immediately:

- Make time to 'switch off' when you are busy or pressured.
- Create some 'me time'.
- Enjoy some relaxing activities.
- Create better work/life balance.

Habit 4 — Time Out for Enjoyable Activities

You have probably heard the saying 'Get a life!' Well if you don't already have one, try the following suggestions. If you have good family relations then make sure you have fun with family time and make time to get to know your kids if you work long hours. If not, socialise with friends over a casual meal, coffee or barbeque for example. Pleasant social activities enhance wellbeing.

Taking up a hobby helps to balance your life and lets you do something you enjoy that is free from the pressure of everyday tasks. It also keeps your brain active. Plan a holiday or a weekend away to get out of the 'rat race' or just to provide a change of environment and some breathing space.

Life often gets too serious, so if something amuses you, share it. A little humour can go a long way to keeping us mentally fit. Contact with animals can also help us emotionally, psychologically, and socially. They provide companionship, safety and comfort through the power of touch. Isolated people without support have been found to have less depression if they have a pet. So have a laugh or try some animal magic.

Balance Action Steps

Start planning how you can:
- Spend time socialising with family or friends.

- Take up a hobby or do some fun activities.
- Take a break or a weekend away.
- Find people or things to make you laugh.

Habit 5 — Positive Thinking

It has been long believed by psychotherapists and counsellors that positive thoughts can help create positive outcomes. It is reassuring that recent information on brain plasticity supports this contention. Accordingly, it is very important to take control of your internal self-talk and learn to change negative thoughts to positive ones.

While they might seem true in the moment, be aware that many thoughts are not reality, they are just a product of your mind and may not be helpful. See *Chapter 5: Throw Out Negative Thoughts* to find out more.

If you are struggling with thinking positively, just keep at it and with practise you will eventually succeed. Keep in mind that research has shown that optimists live 20% longer and cope better with stress, conflict, uncertainty and change. Positive thinking is a powerful aid to good health, good luck and happiness!

Balance Action Steps

You may find you need some help or encouragement to achieve these very important changes. Start to:

- Practice positive self-talk.
- Get rid of negativity.
- Become more optimistic.
- Decide what will make you happier.

Read on to find strategies for achieving these goals.

Beware the Barrier Trap

Many of us are resistant to making changes and often find the concept overwhelming at first. We can feel threatened by what we need to change and see it as a criticism of our very being. We are usually very good at coming up with barriers or obstacles to potential changes.

We might say to ourselves for example:

- It is just too hard.
- It won't work.
- Why should I **have** to change?
- It isn't fair.
- Why isn't there a simple solution?
- I'll start next week.

What do you usually tell yourself? Be honest in your self evaluation.

Self-Motivate with Small Rewards

Evidence shows that it can be motivating to give yourself some rewards for your achievements. If you plan these ahead of time you have something to look forward to. A reward can be tangible such as a new book or CD, a piece of clothing or jewellery, or even an outing.

Alternatively, it can simply be a mental pat on the back or you may just want to share the positive change with a friend who you know will be supportive of you.

Balance Action Steps

Really think critically about your own physical and mental fitness. Write down under each heading of the 'Five Habits' one obstacle that gets in the way of you succeeding in this area. Next reflect on what you can do to overcome what is blocking you. List some self-rewards for overcoming these barriers.

When every physical and mental resource is focused, one's power to solve a problem multiplies tremendously.

Norman Vincent Peale

Replay

- Maintaining both physical and mental fitness keeps us healthy and alive.
- Eat regular healthy meals each day, don't skip meals.
- Regular exercise is important.
- Take time out to have fun and enjoyment.
- Passive relaxation counteracts the stress response.
- Positive thinking helps you live longer and cope better with stress, conflict and change.

Remember to pick one action from this chapter to include in the **Personal Action Planner** at the end of the book.

Chapter 3

Sleep Soundly

How to get a good night's sleep

Dance Step: Ballet

Ballet serves as a backbone for many other styles of dance. It draws people with its smooth gliding motions and uses music and dance to tell a story

How well do you sleep?

Insomnia is the bane of countless people's lives. How often have you suffered a poor night's sleep? How frequently do you hear people say 'I am just not sleeping well at the moment' or 'I am so tired in the mornings from lack of sleep'?

Sleep can be an elusive process when we are worried or anxious. In this day and age our lives are structured such that we often don't get time to ourselves and bedtime becomes the first opportunity to think about ourselves without distractions. Many of us have a tendency towards rumination. This is an anxiety provoking and frustrating tendency to spin thoughts and feelings around and around and constantly over-analyse problems, which can create endless worrying.

A ruffled mind makes a restless pillow.

Charlotte Brontë

Insomnia is so common it has been categorised as a new form of disorder with 20 types of known sleep disorders. Research has shown that difficulty going to sleep is often a sign of anxiety and waking up early and being unable to go back to sleep can be indicative of depression. Middle of the night wakefulness after initially falling asleep can be either one or the other, or it can be due to current stress.

On average it takes just over 20 minutes to fall asleep. One of the common problems with insomnia is lying there worrying about not sleeping and being unable to function during the next day. Yet rest is the next best thing to sleep and lying quietly in the dark can be very restful. If you can calm your mind and stop worrying about not being asleep and rest peacefully, you may very well then fall asleep.

Good sleepers don't think about anything when they go to bed. This doesn't mean that they don't have any problems, but that they have boundaries on when to focus on these problems. For them bedtime is just about sleeping.

Sleep is the best meditation.
                                The Dalai Lama

Why we need a good night's sleep

Sleep is important not only for rest and rejuvenation but also for supporting the immune system. When we sleep, this system is replenished and strengthened so losing even one night of sleep can significantly suppress the immune system. If this happens frequently our health can suffer and we are unable to function at our best.

Lack of sleep causes people to be short tempered and irritable. They perform poorly at work, struggle with effective decision making and problem solving, and often make mistakes. Both professional and personal relationships can be adversely affected.

Latest research has shown that tiredness when driving can have similar effects to driving under the influence of alcohol and drugs. Lack of sleep has also been suggested as a cause of increasing teenage depression.

Learn strategies to sleep better

The good news is that you can learn sleep management skills. Your first goal should be to develop a pattern of sleeping longer hours and to get on a schedule. It takes around 10 weeks to change your circadian rhythm — your 24 hour sleep cycle — and a consistent approach is critical for this to happen. You need to go to bed at the same time each night and try to sleep for the same length of time. Just persevere until you have finally managed it.

All too often we suffer from pre-sleep arousal which can lead to worry and insomnia. Therefore, we need to disconnect bedtime and problem solving as it can trigger mental arousal and lead to physical arousal. In such cases it is important to use mind clearing strategies such as writing down any worries or necessary activities for the next day before attempting to go to sleep. Using a relaxation or meditation CD can help induce sleep.

Alternatively a self-hypnosis sleep strategy can help to calm the mind and encourage sleep. For example, recalling a time or place when you felt very comfortable and relaxed and gradually slowing down your thoughts and relaxing your body as you imagine yourself there.

Tips for better sleeping

To get to sleep

Before going to bed:

- Avoid vigorous exercise or eating as it will stimulate you.
- Don't watch a horror movie or use your computer/tablet/smartphone around two hours before bedtime.
- Have a warm shower or bath.
- Have a hot milky drink or a calming herbal tea.
- Relax peacefully in a comfortable and quiet room for 30 minutes or so.
- Play a relaxation/meditation CD before going to bed, or do so once you are in bed.

To stay asleep

- If you are a poor sleeper, keep your bedroom just for sleeping so don't eat, work or watch TV in bed.
- If you are a worrier, spend some time before going to bed by clearing your mind. Write down everything that is concerning you or that you need to do the following day.
- If light bothers you, wear a sleeping mask.
- If noise bothers you, wear ear plugs.

- If your partner disturbs you, use the guest room or couch until you are sleeping better.

To go back to sleep

- If you wake up in the night with racing thoughts, get up and write down what is bothering you or write a list of what you need to do next day if that is stressing you.
- Calm your mind by listening to a relaxation CD.
- Use a meditation/relaxation process where you progressively relax your muscles and then go to a peaceful place in your mind.
- Sometimes reading will make you sleepy but make sure it is not a highly stimulating book.

Balance Action Steps

Think about your own sleep pattern. Do you need more sleep? Do you need a better sleeping routine? With the above tips in mind, write down five strategies you can adopt to help you sleep better and put them into action from tonight. Keep in mind you will be enhancing your immune system by sleeping better, thus creating better general health. The body repairs while it sleeps.

Issues to consider

Avoid excessive alcohol consumption to help you sleep as it will practically guarantee middle of the night wakefulness. As the alcohol which has helped you to fall into a deep sleep breaks down, it metabolises into a stimulant which will then keep you awake. (Ironic isn't it?)

Sleeping tablets, while usually achieving the goal of sleep, can be very addictive and may lose their effectiveness as you become desensitised to them, thus requiring a stronger and stronger dosage. Some people find that strong sleeping medication makes it difficult to think clearly and function normally the next morning until the effects wear off fully. It may be better to try natural products or a sleep inducing hot drink.

Recent research has compared sleeping medication and Cognitive Behaviour Therapy or CBT (a common form of therapy used to assist people to think and act more productively). The results indicated that CBT is more effective at improving sleep patterns which then stay improved.

Balance Action Steps

Here are two CBT strategies to help you sleep better:

1. Download before bedtime.

    Before you go to bed write down any worries and concerns that have been bothering you recently. This can help clear your mind and allow you to sleep better.

2. Free up the future.

    Write a 'To Do' list of upcoming future activities and tasks that you may be worrying about before going to sleep. This will help clear your mind and reduce any stress associated with what is outstanding.

Hypnosis can help you sleep better

Hypnosis with a properly qualified therapist can also be very effective in improving the ability to sleep. It can reduce anxiety which causes racing thoughts or physical tension.

Hypnosis will also help you learn to relax and to 'tune' out disturbing distractions.

Balance Action Steps

Next time you want to get to sleep more easily, try this self hypnosis sleep strategy. If you can't remember it all, try recording it and playing it when you go to bed.

Make sure you are lying comfortably and quietly in your bed. Take several deep breaths. Close your eyes and concentrate on the sound of your breathing. Continue to take slow, easy breaths while you go through a progressive muscle relaxation technique from your toes to your head.

Tell yourself to relax your feet, calves, knees and thighs. You may feel some heaviness in your legs. Keep breathing slowly and deeply.

Then progressively tell yourself to relax your bottom, abdomen, stomach, back, chest, shoulders and neck, upper arms, elbows, forearms, hands, wrists and fingers. Now move up to the face and loosen up your jaws, cheeks, around your eyes, your forehead and scalp. Your body should now be much more relaxed and you may even feel as if you are sinking into your bed.

Next, keeping your eyes closed and still breathing quite deeply take yourself to a nice relaxing place. Imagine you are really there, on a beach, in a beautiful garden or a rain forest, by a lake or river, walking in the countryside or any other relaxing place that you can bring to mind. Imagine the sights, colours and sounds, the temperature and even the scents or smells of the place. Some people can't see mental pictures but can readily imagine relaxing sounds or create relaxation such as a feeling of floating. Just do whatever works best for you.

By this time your pulse rate and blood pressure will be lowered and your muscles more relaxed. This process allows you to release body tension and 'switch off' your mind and will help you go to sleep or get back to sleep.

Give it a try. You will get better and better at it with practice.

Sleep is the golden chain that ties health and our bodies together

Thomas Dekker

 **Replay**

- Keep your bedroom just for sleeping.
- Avoid excessive stimulation before going to bed.
- Set aside time during the day to think/problem solve so it is not left until bedtime.
- Keep worry out of your bed.
- Use relaxation or meditation CDs to relax your body and calm your mind.
- Practice self-hypnosis strategies to help you sleep.

Remember to pick one action from this chapter to include in the Personal Action Planner at the end of the book.

Chapter 4

Throw Out Negative Thoughts

How to think more positively

Dance Step: The Tango

As the saying goes 'it takes two to tango' with one person leading the other. This dance is often associated with sadness or tragic love.

We all have an internal voice that comes from our subconscious mind and very often sabotages our thinking. This is known as negative self-talk and it includes our conscious thoughts as well as our unconscious assumptions or beliefs.

What is self-talk?

It has been established by psychologists and neuroscientists that every person in the world carries on an ongoing dialogue, or self-talk, of between 150 and 300 words a minute. This works out to between 45,000 and 51,000 thoughts a day. Sounds incredible doesn't it?

It is estimated that approximately 70% percent of all self-talk is negative. Therefore, when we're feeling vulnerable or 'down', our thoughts can become primarily negative.

How does negative self-talk affect us?

Keep in mind that life is not always the way we want it to be. Our plans don't always come to fruition and people often disappoint or hurt us. We don't always succeed at our goals and we often feel let down or like a failure. You need to be aware that it is not actually the situation itself that causes us to feel unhappy, it is the message we give ourselves or what we think about the situation that actually causes our negativity and how upset we become. The way we interpret events has a huge impact on the way we feel and behave.

Negative self-talk can cause us to feel down or bad and to experience upsetting emotions such as hurt, anger, frustration, depression or anxiety. It can also make us behave in a self-defeating way. For instance, thoughts such as 'I'm going to fail for sure' may discourage you from working hard when you are preparing for your exams.

Sometimes we can make ourselves feel pretty unhappy even when our situation is not that dire simply by thinking in a negative, self-defeating way. The problem with self-talk is that it always feels true. Even though your thoughts might often be biased or incorrect, you tend to assume that they're facts when they're actually perceptions.

> *What we think about ourselves becomes the truth for us... Each one of us creates our experiences by our thoughts and our feelings.*
> **Louise Hay**

Become aware of your self-talk

Next time you are feeling down, stop and listen to what you are actually telling yourself. Perhaps write it down. You may be surprised at how negative and self-sabotaging your thoughts can be.

Thoughts you might have could include:
- 'I can't do that.'
- 'It's too hard.'
- 'Why does this always happen to me?'
- 'It's not fair.'
- 'If I say that they will think I'm stupid.'
- 'I look terrible.'

So what do you do about it?

Well, first it is important to remind yourself that the thoughts are **ONLY** thoughts and that they are **NOT** reality so that what you are thinking is not necessarily the truth. Remember, it is only your mind telling you those things. Unfortunately our mind is not always our friend. When we are sad or down it can play tricks on us and sabotage us with negativity.

Secondly, while you may not be able to stop the thoughts coming, it is possible to acknowledge them and then let them go without a struggle. Sit with them and experience them briefly if you wish but don't dwell on them, and then send them away.

A strategy is to imagine you have a river in your mind. Create a positive thought about the situation and send the negative thoughts floating away down the river with the positive thoughts nudging them along. You could also imagine the negative thoughts floating off in a balloon or being blown away by the breeze. Then replace the unhelpful thought with one that is more positive and make a commitment to positive action or if that doesn't work, find a useful distraction.

Thirdly, focus on the here and now or the immediate future. Keep repeating a new positive self-statement over and over again just like a mantra in order to reprogram your subconscious mind. This will start to change your thinking. Once you are practiced at this and it comes naturally, you can tailor your thoughts to specific situations. Keep reminding yourself that even though you can't always control the situation you're in, you **can** change the way you think about it.

When you first start practicing these strategies, you may wish to create some general positive thoughts or self-statements to replace the negative ones. New thoughts could include things such as:

- 'I am confident and happy.'
- 'I can do that.'
- 'I am a good person.'
- 'I am healthy and successful.'
- 'I will stay calm in the interview.'

Balance Action Steps

Practice contradicting your negative thoughts to stop self-sabotage

When you are feeling sad, angry or unhappy, write down your negative thoughts in a note book. You may be surprised at how self-sabotaging they are. Next draw a line down the middle of the page and write a contradictory statement for each one. Keep doing this and you will find that with practise you are gradually able to change any negative thinking.

Chapter 4 Throw Out Negative Thoughts

> *Dwelling on the negative simply contributes to its power.*
>
> **Shirley Maclaine**

It is important to work on putting the thoughts into action so as to create changes in your behaviour. Remember though that your thoughts are always the starting point.

Thoughts affect feelings, which then affect behaviour. Don't be fooled into thinking that you can easily change your actions without also changing what you are thinking.

Balance Action Steps

Try the 4Cs Method

CAPTURE the thought. Awareness is the key, so when you feel 'down', listen to what you are saying. It can be helpful to write it down.

CHALLENGE the thought. Who said that you are not good enough? Why can't you do something? Where is it all coming from? You will find that it is an internal process and it is useful to challenge yourself if you can and notice that these thoughts are coming from within.

CONTROL the thought. While you can't stop negative thoughts as they are automatic, you can send them away. As in the previous example, acknowledge them, sit with them briefly and then send them off in a format that works best for you.

CHANGE the thought. While we might find it hard to ignore our thoughts, as indicated we can send them away as not being helpful. With practice, you will be able to replace negative thoughts with positive thoughts, initially using a general self-statement. Eventually with practice, you will be able to come up with a whole range of different and more positive thoughts that apply to each specific situation.

Positive outcomes through action

If you keep practicing the 4Cs method, you will become better and better at managing and changing your thought processes. But remember, positive thinking alone is not enough, though it is a very great help and can start off the change process.

Once you are thinking more positively, you will develop more confidence to put those thoughts into action. Once you are feeling more confident about yourself, then you can actually start doing things differently.

Give it a try; you may be pleasantly surprised at how well it works. Remember the old proverb, 'If at first you don't succeed, try, try again'.

> *Once you replace negative thoughts with positive ones, you'll start having positive results.*
> **Willie Nelson**

Chapter 4 Throw Out Negative Thoughts

Replay

- Most of our self-talk is negative.
- It is a not the event itself but our negative interpretation that causes us to feel bad.
- Remind yourself that thoughts are ONLY thoughts and that they are often NOT true.
- Acknowledge negative thoughts, sit briefly with them and then let them go without a struggle. Keep practising until you can do this effectively.
- Replace with a positive thought and commit to positive action or find a useful distraction
- Try the 4Cs method to help you think more positively.

Remember to pick one action from this chapter to include in the **Personal Action Planner** at the end of the book.

Chapter 5

Stay Stress Savvy

How to manage life's stressors

Dance Step: The Cha Cha

Cha Cha can be both delicate and emotional. People are powerfully attracted to dancing Cha Cha possibly because of the catchy and light rhythm or the carefree and non-hurried feel of the dance.

What is actually meant by 'stress'?

Everyday life is full of pressure and we all experience it from time to time. We need to be mindful though that it is not the pressure itself, but how we manage it that impacts on how we cope with it. Some people say stress is all in the mind but, as indications are that a very large percentage of presenting symptoms at the GP are stress-related, clearly this is not so.

The Oxford Dictionary definition of stress is:

A state of mental or emotional strain or tension resulting from adverse or demanding circumstances.

Unfortunately the term stress is commonly bandied about by anybody who feels they are under a level of pressure with which they are having difficulty coping. As a result it is frequently misused in many settings.

Similarly, stress is typically seen as a negative concept impacting on both the mind and body despite it being a very normal and necessary part of being alive and mostly manageable. A small amount of stress is what gets us moving on a daily basis. It is only when we experience too much stress over too long a period that it starts to become a problem.

Stress can be considered an internal factor — if you subject 10 people to the same stressful circumstance you will see 10 completely different coping responses. Some people will cope well and 'bounce back', others will become 'distressed'. It all depends on how they perceive the situation and how strong their coping ability is.

The Stress Response

```
        PRESSURE
         | | |
         STRESS
        /      \
APPROPRIATE OR   DISTRESS!
COPING RESPONSE
```

How does stress impact on us?

Stress can affect us both at work and home. Be aware that all stress is not bad stress. There is "eustress" or good stress (a term credited to endocrinologist Hans Selye) which is desirable or appropriate stress and which keeps us motivated and moving. If we experience no stress at all, we can become very lazy and apathetic, but if we are constantly subjected to large amounts of stress then it can negatively impact on our performance, our health and our behaviour. Stress which is ignored can result over time in anxiety.

Stress burnout is probably the biggest cost for businesses. While we can often cope in the short-term, it's the long-term effects that damage our self-esteem, relationships and health, and affect our work performance.

Stages and Effects of Stress

Stress tends to come in three stages.

Stage 1 — Alarm

This is known as the **fight or flight** response, which creates:

- Increased respiration.
- Increased heart rate.
- Increased blood pressure.
- Increased muscle tension.
- Increased adrenalin.

This stage causes a physiological effect that we have retained from our ancestors or from 'cave man' times. This is the response that you experience when you fear danger, or have to do something which you find stressful. For example, it can occur with a near miss in the car, when you have a conflict with somebody, or when you have to stand up and make a speech in front of a group of people.

Your heart may pound, your mouth might become dry, you can become shaky and sweaty, and sometimes you feel a choking sensation in your throat or chest. However, once the adrenaline subsides, this effect will reduce. You just need to give it time.

Stage 2 — Resistance

In this stage, there are many early warning signals. We will all experience some of them some of the time, but if we find we are experiencing a lot of them a lot of the time, then we need to take action to deal with what is happening.

It is important to take notice of whether you are experiencing a number of **early warning signals**, as ignoring them can lead to more serious health or behavioural issues. Some these include:

- backaches
- indigestion
- gritting teeth
- clenching jaw
- clenching hands
- knotted stomach
- clamminess
- fatigue
- sleep disturbances
- headaches
- shortness of breath
- frequent colds/infections
- skin problems
- irritability
- anxiety and tension for more than a day or two
- poor concentration
- unexplained nausea
- loss of appetite
- overeating
- diarrhoea
- mouth ulcers
- increased consumption of drugs or alcohol
- sadness
- withdrawal

Stage 3 — Exhaustion

The reactions at this stage have much longer term effects. If you have ever had a friend or family member family who has experienced a 'break down' you will be aware of how difficult it is for them to recover from this. So prevention is paramount. Just as we need to keep our cars maintained to keep them running if we don't look after our minds and bodies then we can suffer both physical and emotional effects.

Physical effects of stage 3 stress exhaustion include:

- stroke
- migraine
- asthma
- arthritis
- cancer
- heart attack
- stomach ulcers
- back problems
- intense chest pains
- high blood pressure

Emotional effects of stage 3 stress exhaustion include:

- anxiety
- depression
- trauma
- sexual problems
- low self-confidence
- low self-esteem
- relationship problems
- performance problems
- withdrawal
- suicide

It is not stress that kills us it is our reaction to it.
Hans Selye (known as the 'Father of stress')

Balance Action Steps

Try this quick Stress Assessment to check on whether you are stressed at the moment.

Examine the following list of stress symptoms. Then think about how frequently you have experienced any of these over the last month or so.

Use the following key for scoring:

   0 = hardly ever

   1 = occasionally (once every two to four weeks)

   2 = sometimes (once or twice every one or two weeks)

   3 = often (every second or third day)

   4 = very often (every day)

Symptoms of Stress Quiz

Mood
I feel nervous	0	1	2	3	4
I worry excessively	0	1	2	3	4
I have difficulty concentrating	0	1	2	3	4
I feel generally irritable	0	1	2	3	4

Behaviour
I become withdrawn	0	1	2	3	4
I am short tempered with others	0	1	2	3	4
I have difficulty going to sleep	0	1	2	3	4
I wake up frequently in the night	0	1	2	3	4

Organs
I feel my heart pounding	0	1	2	3	4
I breathe rapidly	0	1	2	3	4
My stomach becomes upset	0	1	2	3	4
I perspire easily	0	1	2	3	4

Muscles
I cannot sit or stand still	0	1	2	3	4
My muscles are tense and stiff	0	1	2	3	4
I clench my jaw or grind my teeth	0	1	2	3	4
I feel very fatigued	0	1	2	3	4

What should your stress symptoms scores show?

Ideally you will have scores of 1 or 2 for most areas. If you have all zeros you may be almost comatose. However, if you have a lot of 3's and especially 4's then you definitely need to do something about your stress levels to prevent mental or physical health problems.

How to combat personal stress

One of the most effective ways to deal with stress is to learn effective coping mechanisms. This will strengthen you emotionally and will help to boost your immune system. Revisit Chapter 2 for a refresher on the '**Five Habits**', which include:

1. Healthy eating.
2. Regular exercise and sufficient sleep.
3. Time out for relaxing activities.
4. Time out for enjoyable activities.
5. Positive thinking and overcoming negative thoughts.

Seek help if it is needed

If you can't manage this by yourself then make sure you seek advice from a qualified person or gain professional help to learn appropriate coping skills. Ask your doctor for a referral to a psychologist or stress management expert.

Stress at Work

Workplace stress is occurring more and more in our busy society as resources are reduced, and yet the workload remains the same or increases. Workplace stress can be defined as an emotional experience and includes nervousness, tension and strain due to work-related factors.

Recent statistics indicate that workplace stress:

- costs the Australian economy $14.81 billion a year, and directly costs Australian employers $10.11 billion a year,
- loses employers 3.2 days per worker each year, and
- has doubled the number of stress related claims in the last 15 years.

Ways of dealing with workplace stress

Create a pleasing work environment

If you have the power to do so, paint the walls in soft colours or play music while working. Other things you can do are to introduce fresh flowers, plants, fish tanks, bright pictures or posters to your work space and personalise it with a photograph or two.

Create a healthy work environment

Many organisations are now introducing outside professionals to run lunch time sessions of yoga or massage, for example. If your workplace has such options sign up. If not, then it might be helpful to organise an exercise group who can go walking together or a group who can do activities such as yoga or tai chi.

Get away from your desk

If you have one, use the tea room for morning, afternoon tea or lunch, or go for a walk outside if possible.

Utilise your employee assistance program (EAP)

This service is offered by most companies to be of assistance if you are struggling.

Quick tips to de-stress your job

Take regular short 'time out' breaks and clear your head

This will help you focus better and be more effective at problem solving and decision making.

Make jobs that have to be done a priority and do less urgent ones when there's time

We frequently have too much to do so it is important to cut out distractions and by tackling priority jobs first, we'll feel less stressed in getting them done. However, if you're feeling tired, angry or unwell then it is probably not the best time to make important decisions or undertake problem-solving of a critical nature.

Organise your thoughts and take deep breaths before making a difficult call or seeing a difficult client

We all have to deal with colleagues, customers and bosses who can be difficult at times. If we calm ourselves with some deep breathing and are clear on what we wish to discuss, then when we actually speak to them or see them in person, we will approach it in a calmer and more organised manner. This in turn will help us deal with any negative responses they are likely to make.

Buy yourself time by not saying 'yes' automatically

It is important to realise that we do not have to jump every time somebody asks us to. A useful reply to a request for extra work is to say 'Let me check and get back to you'. This will then allow you to decide how you wish to respond or gather information that is required without becoming stressed.

Avoid putting unrealistic pressure on yourself

Accept that you can't know everything and ask for help if you feel overwhelmed or overloaded. Go to your boss and let them know that you can't meet unrealistic deadlines. It is not a weakness to ask for help but rather is a sensible course of action.

Balance Action Steps

Commit to doing at least one of the above actions and share it with a friend or colleague to ensure accountability. Either change your environment, your attitude or your behaviour and see what occurs. Don't just stop at one!

Fast and Funky Stress Busters

Here are some simple, effective and fun strategies to reduce stress. Give them a try.

Eat dark chocolate

Don't forget what Swiss scientists call the 'chocolate cure'. A clinical trial in Lausanne found that eating 40 grams of dark chocolate daily for two weeks reduced the stress hormone cortisol in people who reported feeling 'highly stressed'. Unfortunately for the 'chocoholics', eating more chocolate won't further reduce stress — around 40 grams a day seems to be the right amount.

Snack on walnuts

Research from Pennsylvania State University in US found that a handful of walnuts daily (about 18 walnut halves) helps lower stress related blood pressure. Walnuts contain fibre, antioxidants and omega-3 fatty acids which have a positive effect on blood pressure.

Chew gum

Something as simple as chewing a stick of gum can help relieve mild to moderate stress. It can also make you more alert and help you multi-task, say researchers from Melbourne's Swinburne University and the Wrigley Science Institute in Chicago. They found that anxiety levels dropped by 17% in mildly stressed people when they chewed gum.

Hum a tune

Thinking of a favourite song and spending a minute or two humming a few verses can halt the stress cycle for a while. Apparently humming helps relax tense muscles, blocks out the thoughts racing around our heads and makes sure we breathe more deeply and calmly. The result is a moment of peace.

Blow up a balloon

The act of blowing up a balloon does two important things for stress relief: it makes you breathe more deeply because you have to use your diaphragm, and it makes you breathe more slowly. Both these things activate our parasympathetic nervous system, which reduces our heart rate and relaxes our muscles.

Reducing Stress: You can do it!

Keep in mind the saying 'If it's meant to be it's up to me'. You have the power to create and maintain strong personal resources so that even if you face high levels of stress or pressure, you will be able to cope and move forward because you will be in 'eustress'. If you can't manage this by yourself then make sure you seek advice from an expert or seek professional help to learn coping skills.

If you allow your resources to weaken in the face of adversity or high stress you may implode and go into the 'Distress' state (revisit **Stages and Effects of Stress:** *Stage 3* to remind you of the symptoms).

The graph below shows the relationship between low personal resources and stress.

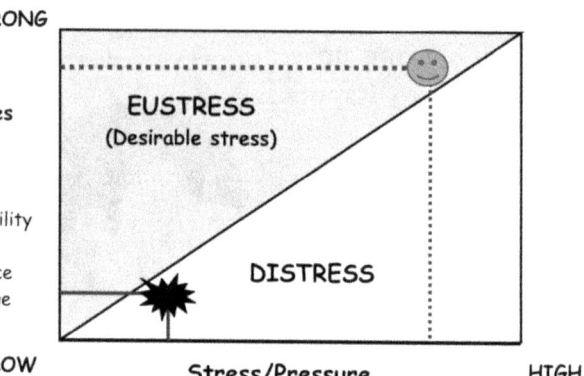

If you ask what is the single most important key for longevity, I would have to say it is avoiding worry, stress and tension.

George Burns

Replay

- Remember that stress is a normal part of being alive
- Managing stress depends on your mental attitude and strength of coping skills
- Take note of early warning signals
- Learn to deal with workplace stress
- Build up your personal resources to avoid burnout
- If you can't manage it on your own then seek professional help.

Remember to pick one action from this chapter to include in the **Personal Action Planner** at the end of the book.

Chapter 6

Face Your Fears

How to alleviate anxiety

> *Dance Step: The Swing (Also called Jitterbug or Boogie Woogie)*
>
> A lively dance style which expresses a variety of emotions. A song 'swings' because when dancers hear it they can't stand still.

What causes anxiety?

Life itself is the ultimate cause of many of our emotional problems. Health, relationships, work, finances, children and aging parents can all create anxiety.

Anxiety is one of the most common human emotional states there is. It is a normal response and relates to the physical, mental and behavioural changes that occur with stress or danger. For example, if you were being chased by a wild animal, these automatic changes would cause you to either run for your life or become sufficiently energised to try to physically defend yourself. This is the 'flight or fight' response.

Anxiety can also be experienced in unfamiliar situations such as a job interview, exam, first date, large social gathering etc. Before competing, athletes will usually experience some anxiety which serves to 'pump' them up and get them ready to do their best.

When anxiety becomes a problem

Have you ever felt overwhelmed by a major problem or even several smaller problems? Have you ever felt that you have lost your normal ability to cope? This is usually due to anxiety.

Anxiety becomes a problem when it is so extreme that it stops you from taking action or it interferes with your activities, your work and your life. If you feel highly stressed about something and as if you have lost all control of a situation, then anxiety can occur as a result.

> *Anxiety, it just stops your life.*
> **Amanda Seyfried**

Common types of anxiety responses include the following:

Generalised anxiety disorder which causes:
- Continuous anxiety and inability to get to a completely relaxed state.
- Excessive and persistent worry about a number of areas of life.

Panic disorder which causes:
- Recurrent and often unexpected panic attacks.
- Extreme and intense anxiety and sometimes a wish to 'escape'.
- Fear of having another panic attack or what people will think if this occurs.

Social anxiety or **phobia** which causes:
- Anxiety about being judged or watched closely by others.
- Avoidance of certain situations (for example social activities, shopping malls).

Watch your self-talk

People who experience anxiety and panic attacks are especially prone to listen to their negative self-talk. What they say to themselves about a situation directly determines how they feel and how they react. The level of anxiety felt is due to how they interpret events. In other words, negative thoughts cause bad feelings which then result in fearful or negative behaviour such as avoidance, wanting to escape and sometimes repeated ritual behaviour.

Don't believe those automatic thoughts

Thoughts have power. During times of anxiety negative automatic thoughts will pop into your head. These can dominate your thinking and, as a result, your feelings and emotions. We tend to believe these thoughts even if they are not true, which they usually aren't. It is just your mind playing mean tricks on you. Be aware that in times of stress your mind is not always your friend. The messages it sends you can sabotage your coping mechanisms and cause negative reactions.

Your thinking is not necessarily wrong when you are experiencing an intense feeling or mood, but you are much more likely to distort, ignore or disregard contradictory information to your feelings or beliefs at such times.

Everyone thinks like this at times and these thoughts are usually automatic. Learn to recognise when you are thinking in negative, unhelpful and distorted ways. Recognising you are doing this is the first step toward having more balanced thinking and feelings. (Revisit Chapter 4)

Strategies to Help Reduce Anxiety

Anxious feelings can be very unpleasant or uncomfortable so obviously we want to try to reduce or stop them. People often think that there is nothing they can do about it — but don't despair. While you may not be able to get rid of anxiety entirely, there is a whole range of positive practical steps that can be taken to help manage it.

While it may not always be obvious, remember that for most people there are solutions to problems, even if they are temporary ones. Be aware that anxiety is a signal to start thinking about what might be wrong in your way of life and what action you need to take to overcome it.

1. Do a Reality Check

Sometimes actually having anxiety makes it hard to take action and some people will run away from their problems or become reclusive as it is all 'too hard' to cope with. At times like this it is useful to do a '**reality check**'.

Balance Action Steps

Think of something which is causing you anxiety and try this reality check:

- Stand back from the problem to see more clearly what action you could take.
- Talk to family and friends to get their perspective.
- Take time out to take your mind off of it, for example an evening out, a weekend break or a holiday.
- Be aware of any changes in your thinking.
- Seek professional help if these things don't work.

---

2. Seek Support from Others

There is an old proverb that says 'a problem shared is a problem halved'. A friendly sympathetic ear from family or friends is well recognised to help overcome problems.

Sometimes opening up about your problems can help to clarify them and allow you to see what you need to do.

Some people don't like to interact with anyone at all when they are feeling really anxious but it is very important not to cut yourself off from other people. Often just a short chat may really help, but avoid anyone who is unsympathetic or over critical as they may make matters worse.

Often anxious people worry about burdening others with their problems and tend to keep to themselves. Ask yourself this. If you had a friend who needed help and came to you, what would your reaction be? More than likely you would want to help. They are also likely to feel that way too, but make sure you don't overwhelm them.

Interestingly, often when we disclose our feelings, we find others who are experiencing the same thing but haven't felt comfortable to say so. Your self-disclosure will give them permission to share their issues with you. You may be surprised how many people will 'come out of the woodwork' with their own problems. You can then mutually support each other if appropriate.

3. Use Breathing Techniques

Deep, slow breathing helps control any hyperventilation (rapid breathing that comes with anxiety) and other symptoms of anxiety. The rate of breathing when feeling calm or relaxed is around 10 breaths per minute. Generally, when we breathe we either use 'chest or abdominal-breathing'.

If you are troubled by nerves, worries and anxiety in life, chances are you're a 'chest-breather'. Chest-breathers may experience breath-holding, hyperventilation, shortness of breath, or fear of fainting.

'Abdominal-breathing' is deeper and steadier and is a smooth and even way of breathing. It maintains the balance of oxygen and carbon dioxide in the blood, allowing the body and brain to function effectively.

Action Steps for Better Balance

Breathing exercise

Use this exercise as soon as any feelings of anxiety or panic start. Combining slow breathing with relaxation is particularly effective. You need to practice this exercise several times a day for it to be most effective.

1. Place your hands at the bottom of your rib cage and pay attention to your breathing.
2. Close your eyes, hold your breath and count to 5 (don't take in a deep breath).
3. When you get to 5, breathe out and say the word *relax* to yourself in a calm, soothing way.
4. Breathe in and out slowly through your nose. Breathe in for 3 seconds and out for 3 seconds. As you breathe in, imagine you are sending your breath as far down into your body as it will go. As you breathe out, imagine all the tension in your body leaving with your breath as you say the word *relax* to yourself every time you breathe out. You should notice your abdomen rising and falling with your hand as your lungs expand as they fill up with air.
5. Keeping your eyes closed continue to gently breathe in this way, in and out through your nose. At rest, breathing through your nose is more efficient. Breathe slowly, the slower the better.
6. Now keeping your eyes closed, place your arms at your side if standing, or on your lap if sitting. Breathe in and out through

your nose. If your breathing feels unnatural or forced in any way, just maintain your awareness of that sensation as you continue to breathe in and out. Eventually, any straining or unnaturalness should ease up by itself.
7. Continue breathing in this way until all the symptoms of over breathing or hyperventilation have gone.
8. Concentrate on your breathing. Breathe in and out as your abdomen moves out and in. Notice that your breathing and abdomen move in opposite directions. Don't think of anything but your breathing. Continue this for 5 to 10 minutes and notice how relaxed you feel.

For breath is life, and if you breathe well you will live long on earth

Sanskrit Proverb

4. Use Progressive Muscle Relaxation with Positive Visualisation

This technique is good for both the body and the mind and helps to boost the immune system which results in better health. It is best done in a quiet or peaceful setting with no interruptions.

Firstly you find a comfortable spot and imagine relaxing all muscles of the body in sequence from head to toe or vice versa. You then visualise a calm and peaceful place and imagine being there. This is extremely beneficial when you feel anxious or stressed. If you find it hard to visualise, you can imagine a favourite piece of music or a feeling of floating.

There is extensive research showing that visualisation is an effective tool to help with anxiety. You can also check out the numerous websites which support this and will provide more advice on how to go about it.

5. Practice Positive Self-Statements or Affirmations

One way to counter anxiety provoking negative self-talk is by using positive self-statements or affirmations. Doing this will help you to change negative or mistaken beliefs or thinking by reprogramming your subconscious mind. For example, saying '**I can do xxx**' in relation to something that you don't have the confidence to try or '**I will stay calm**' if feeling anxious about having to talk to a room full of people.

Such affirmations should be short and concise so they can be easily remembered. Writing them down, listening to them recorded on tapes or using constant repetition can result in changing some of the core beliefs that underlie negative self-talk. They work very well in combination with relaxation and visualisation as described above.

Affirmations should be:
- Short, simple and direct.
- Present or future tense for example I am…, I will….
- In the positive.
- Contain a positive change.
- Match some willingness to believe they are possible.

6. Try Meditation

Meditation can help people achieve a sense of calm, focus on things, sleep better, and help with clearer problem solving and decision making. It is also excellent for good health but it does take practice in order to work. It is quite difficult to still our busy minds. Try using a meditation CD or joining a class. The more you practice the easier it becomes.

7. Have a Massage

Massage can be extremely relaxing for both the body and the mind. It can be performed by a professional or by a partner or friend. Generally professional masseurs utilise relaxing music and aromatherapy oils to enhance the experience. For example lavender oil creates a feeling of calm while citrus oils lift the mood. You can use an oil burner at home for the same effect.

If you would like to try a professional massage but can't afford it, consider contacting one of the massage schools who are often seeking willing people for their students to practice on.

When to Seek Professional Help

If you have taken a break from routine and it hasn't worked and no matter how much support you have gained it isn't helping; no matter how much you have worked on your relationships, nothing seems to be working out; you are still feeling highly anxious and you may even be having panic attacks — now it is time to seek professional help.

The first step is to see your GP and have a complete physical examination to make sure there is nothing physically wrong. You may need to take some medication. If you do not want to take prescribed drugs, there are a number of natural medications that can help. See your pharmacist or a naturopath.

You can then ask your GP to refer you to a psychologist who can support you and teach you relaxation techniques and proven practical strategies to manage your anxiety. They are skilled and experienced in assisting people with these issues.

If your anxiety is severe, don't think it will just get better on its own. It usually won't, so be smart and seek professional help.

Don't let your fear of being judged stop you from asking for help when you need it...

Anonymous

Replay

Anxiety is a common human emotional state.

- Manage your self-talk and don't believe your automatic negative thoughts.
- Do a reality check from time to time.
- Seek support from others.
- Use the proven strategies outlined above to help.
- Seek professional help if you are struggling to manage your anxiety.

Remember to pick one action from this chapter to include in the **Personal Action Planner** at the end of the book.

Chapter 7

Break Through the Dark Clouds

How to survive despite depression

Dance Step: Flamenco

Originating from Andalusia in Spain this is a passionate form of dance which is shrouded in mystery. It expresses the deepest and saddest emotions but can also transform into being romantic and entertaining.

What is depression really?

Depression is a serious and complex mood disorder or mental health issue and can sneak up on you as a result of ongoing and unresolved problems in life or at work. Alternatively, it can arise after a deeply upsetting event. It is a common occurrence today and affects about 121 million people worldwide and is spreading. The World Health Organization (WHO) predicts it will be the second greatest cause of human disability in the world by the year 2020.

The Oxford dictionary defines depression as:

> *'A condition characterized by severe feelings of hopelessness and inadequacy, typically accompanied by a lack of energy and interest in life.'*

Depression in Australia

Every year around 6% of all adult Australians are affected by a depressive illness of some kind. More women experience depression than men and, at any point in time, up to 5% of adolescents experience depression that is severe enough to warrant treatment. Around 20% of young people will have experienced significant depressive symptoms by the time they reach adulthood.

Depression can have biological, psychological or social causes. No matter which of these is the origin, it will significantly affect the way you feel, with an ongoing negative impact on your moods. It is often accompanied by a range of other physical and psychological symptoms that get in the way of functioning effectively in everyday life and work. But please take heart if you have depression. The symptoms generally react positively to the right treatment and will frequently resolve over time.

What are the symptoms?

We all know the feeling of being 'down'. This is a normal healthy reaction to a troublesome or difficult life event or work situation. Many of us confuse this with depression. True depression is when these feelings are not in proportion to what has occurred in our external or work life and when the negative feelings and symptoms continue over time.

Depression is often described as a black cloud hanging over one's head. It is perceived as heavy and thick and hard to shift. It is also known as the 'black dog'.

Depression manifests in a lot of different symptoms and affects people in many different ways. Common symptoms include a disturbance in normal sleep patterns, and feeling anxious or bad about yourself. Some people report feeling very sad or teary and can find no pleasure in life. Many become 'snappy' with other people or display a short fuse. Depressed people frequently say that they feel worthless, or hopeless and helpless, and usually 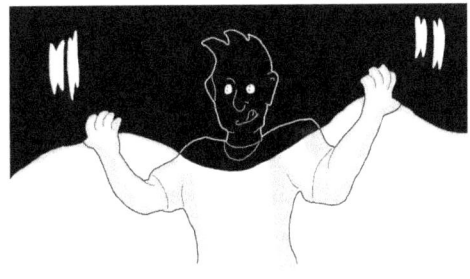 they lose motivation to do much at all. Getting out of bed, going to work, or going out socially or even shopping can be difficult for them.

Physical aches and pains, clouded thinking and loss of sexual interest can occur. Some people experience memory problems and find it hard to concentrate. Others may lose or gain weight. Relationship problems with friends, family or colleagues frequently occur, as does a tendency towards isolation, unusual fears and thoughts of death.

If you have depression you may excessively dwell on your problems with your mind going round and round in circles and continually over-analysing the issues. This is called 'rumination' and is a common symptom.

If you have had several of the above symptoms for a prolonged period you are possibly experiencing depression. If so please see your doctor as soon as possible to discuss what is going on with you. Depending on the seriousness of your situation, you may need a referral on to a suitable psychologist or psychiatrist for assistance, or require appropriate medication.

Warning signs

There are a number of warning signs which will help you recognise that you may be feeling depressed or anxious. Other people may notice some of them and comment to you. It's a good idea to listen and get help before they develop further.

Some of the most common symptoms are:
- Getting up later.
- Finding it hard to concentrate.
- Skipping meals and eating unhealthily.
- Having disturbed sleep.
- Feeling irritable, stressed and teary.
- Withdrawing socially or wanting to spend a lot of time alone.

What causes depression?

Depression can arise from:
- A severe loss or ongoing stress (reactive depression).
- Part of an illness in which the person experiences extreme moods, both extremely up and down, without any apparent reason (bipolar disorder).
- After the birth of a child (post-natal depression).
- A chemical imbalance in the brain (endogenous depression).
- Hormonal changes or disorders.
- A chronically unhealthy lifestyle, with a poor diet and not enough exercise or sleep.

Frequently asked questions about depression

Am I losing my mind?

No you are not. You are suffering symptoms of an illness that can be treated. Many other people experience the same illness and you can stop worrying that you are 'going crazy'.

Is this normal or is it just me?

If you are experiencing the symptoms outlined above then they are common for depression. In other words, they are a normal response to an abnormal situation. With help, over time they will most likely reduce.

Will people think that I'm weak?

Even the strongest people can suffer depression. Just think about all the celebrities who are currently coming out of the woodwork to disclose their experiences. Many are tough action heroes. You don't need to feel embarrassed or ashamed as depression is so common now.

Why can't I snap out of it?

If you break an arm or leg you can't play tennis or run a marathon straight away. You need a recovery period and probably some sort of rehabilitation. Overcoming depression takes time and patience and we know that you will do better if you get help.

> *The greatest glory in living lies not in never failing, but in rising every time we fail.*
>
> **Nelson Mandela**

How is depression treated?

If you have an illness or condition which is life threatening or significantly negatively affects your lifestyle you are more likely to experience symptoms of depression. While some depressive symptoms may be considered a 'normal' response, it is always worth having a chat with your doctor as a depressive illness may have been triggered by other means and need treatment.

Treatment can do much to reduce and even eliminate the symptoms of depression. Treatment may include a combination of medication, individual therapy and support from family or friends.

What sort of treatment will help?

Medication

The drugs most used for depression include anti-depressants, tranquillisers (mostly used to treat psychotic symptoms) and mood stabilizers (used for bipolar disorder). Anti-depressants are the most widely used and vary in their effectiveness. Anti-depressants can be an effective form of treatment for moderate to severe depression but should not be the first line of treatment for cases of mild depression. Please keep in mind that if you are taking anti-depressants and you start to feel better never go off them 'cold turkey' as this can cause a very negative reaction.

An Alternative Viewpoint

Dr Michael Yapko, a clinical psychologist and author of many books about depression, writes in his book *Depression is Contagious* that depression can occur as a result of negative relationships, not just biological factors. He says that while drugs can address some depressive symptoms they do not change the social factors that cause and maintain depression.

Dr Yapko advises that if you have depression you need to be empowered to overcome it by changing your thinking, readjusting your expectations, interacting more positively with others and becoming motivated to improve and strengthen all your relationships. He believes that with the right expert assistance, you will better overcome the depression and are less likely to relapse. He states that this approach will also reduce your children's vulnerability to depression and is a pathway to recovery 'through people not pills'. He presents a number of helpful strategies for self empowerment in his book, *Breaking the Patterns of Depression*.

Other Treatments

Cognitive Behaviour Therapy

This is a noninvasive psychological treatment which can help you change your negative view of yourself and the world. It will show you how your thoughts can affect your thinking and then influence your feelings and will teach you how to correct faulty thinking. Most psychologists utilise this form of treatment in their practice.

Balance Action Steps

Try this technique for stopping self-sabotage

Get yourself a small notebook and carry it with you. When you are feeling sad, angry or unhappy, write down your negative thoughts in your note book. You may be surprised at how self-sabotaging they are. Then draw a line down the middle of the page and write a contradictory statement for each one. Keep doing this and you will find that over time you may gradually be able to change your thinking.

You largely constructed your depression. It wasn't given to you. Therefore, you can deconstruct it.
Albert Ellis, Psychologist and founder of REBT

Hypnotherapy

Hypnotherapy is considered by many to be one of the most useful ways of teaching people to master the skills to overcome depression. It involves self-focus and rebuilding your frame of mind. A skilled practitioner can teach you the skills to overcome anxiety and depression and find some hope for the future. Make sure you see an appropriately qualified professional such as a psychologist if you take this option.

Mindfulness Meditation

This practice involves you in focusing on what is actually happening in the present moment while not analysing or judging what is occurring. It is useful to deal with depression, anxiety and stress. Most practitioners can help you with this approach.

Balance Action Steps

Next time you feel sad or anxious try this mindfulness meditation. Firstly focus on your breath. Listen to the sound of your breathing as you slowly breathe in and out feeling your stomach inflate on the in-breath and deflate on the out-breath. Notice how it feels and how you feel.

See if you can identify the emotion. What word best describes what you are feeling? Is it sad, scared, anxious, angry, frustrated or helpless? Where are you feeling it in your body, for example is it a tightness in your chest, throat, head etc? Now just accept that the emotion is a normal bodily reaction to stress or anxiety. Don't analyse or judge the emotion. Simply let it flow through you without resistance or fighting against it.

If you find that you're having intruding thoughts and start to focus on trying to ignore them or blaming yourself for having them or believing them, just sit quietly with them and focus back on your breathing and to the bodily feelings of the emotion.

When you feel calmer and more detached from the emotion bring yourself back to the present.

Self-help strategies to help with depression

Exercise is excellent

Get active. Research has shown that exercising regularly can increase the level of serotonin, the 'happy hormone' and also

will increase the production of endorphins which can lift moods. Sometimes exercise alone can be equally effective as anti-depressants in treating mild to moderate depression or it will help people who have not responded well to medication.

Physical exercise will definitely help but keep it simple and enjoyable. Try walking, swimming, dancing, playing golf or tennis or going to the gym Try to do some physical exercise every day, even if it's just going for a walk Find an 'exercise buddy' to keep you motivated.

Healthy eating helps

Good nutrition is known to boost your immune system which in turn will help you manage stress, anxiety and depression. Increasing the amount of Omega 3 oils in your diet is beneficial in combating depression and recent research has suggested that reducing sugar in your diet may also help.

Random acts of kindness will boost your mood

Doing good things for others will help you feel better about yourself. When you do such things you are likely to produce hormones that will boost wellbeing. Among other things this can include volunteering, donating to a good cause or simply helping out a neighbour or colleague.

Sonja Lyubomirsky, a psychology professor at the University of California, and her colleagues found that people with a tendency toward depression can help themselves by helping others or otherwise introducing positivity into their day-to-day lives. She writes 'You have to do work. It takes effort to continually remind yourself to do acts of kindness for others, although I think it gets easier over time.' She says more about how to introducing positivity into your life in her book *The How of Happiness*.

Try animal magic

Studies show that animals can reduce tension and improve mood and boost the production of 'feel-good' hormones. Along with treatment, pets can help some people with mild to moderate depression feel better as they offer unconditional love and companionship and seem to be able to tune into when their owners feel down and need comfort.

Taking care of a pet can remind you of your own value and that you are capable when you have lost self-belief. Pets are a great topic of conversation if you feel stuck for words and you may find opportunities to talk to people if you are feeling isolated, such as when you are at the vet. If you have a dog it will get you off the couch to take it for a walk. Studies have shown that petting a dog or cat is good for your heart health too.

Three important things to aim for

1. Cut down alcohol and other drugs

These can cause long-term problems and make it much harder to recover. Avoid stimulants, in particular too much caffeine and recreational drugs, as these make depression and anxiety worse.

2. Recognise your triggers

Common triggers can include a breakdown in relationships with family, friends or colleagues, ongoing work related stress or a major change in your life such as losing your job or moving away from your support group. Chronic health problems or excessive use of alcohol or drugs can also be problematic. If you know that these will trigger the onset of depression, seek help immediately if they occur. Remember prevention is often easier than a cure!

3. Don't despair if you relapse

In the event you have a setback and experience another period of depression, keep in mind that you now have strategies to deal with it and usually the recovery period is shorter a second time round. Don't beat yourself up as this can block your recovery. Seek help immediately to help you get back on track, come to terms with it and start again. Focus on what worked last time and do these things again. Also learn what triggered the setback and what you need to do to stop it happening again.

> *We must accept finite disappointment, but we must never lose infinite hope.*
>
> **Martin Luther King**

What should I do if I have depression?

If you believe that you may be experiencing depression, the first step is to consult your doctor for advice, treatment and referral to someone who can help.

If you have an immediate need for help call (in Australia):

- **Beyond Blue:** 24-hour telephone assistance on 1300224636, www.beyondblue.org.au
- **Lifeline:** 24-hour telephone counselling service on 131114.
- **The Black Dog Institute:** (02)93824530 Email: blackdog@blackdog.org.au, www.blackdoginstitute.org.au

 **Replay**

- If you think you may be depressed check out the symptoms and warning signs.
- Don't feel embarrassed or ashamed about depression.
- Use proven self-help strategies.
- Recognise your triggers and seek assistance before depression takes hold.
- Don't beat yourself up if it reoccurs.
- Seek help immediately if you need it.

Remember to pick one action from this chapter to include in the **Personal Action Planner** at the end of the book.

Chapter 8

When the Going Gets Tough...

How to build resilience to beat stress

Dance Step: Hip Hop

Improvisation and personal interpretation are essential to hip-hop dancing. It includes a wide range of styles and consists of moves executed primarily close to the ground.

What do we really mean by resilience?

How good are you at 'bouncing back' from difficulties? That's what resilience is all about. Life is getting tougher. There are worldwide financial crises, wars, starvation and infringement on human rights. Protests against tyranny are increasing, religious differences are stronger and people are dying as a result.

On a day-to-day basis we all seem to be living busier and busier lives with more stress and pressure on us. It is becoming more expensive to live, families and friends are more demanding and jobs are harder to find and keep.

Resilience is all about survival. If we work on building our personal resilience we will better survive stressful events and high pressure situations that we find ourselves facing, both in our daily lives and in our workplaces.

The Oxford Dictionary definition of resilience is:

> *'The capacity to recover quickly from difficulties, prolonged toughness'.*

There are four areas in which we can build resilience.

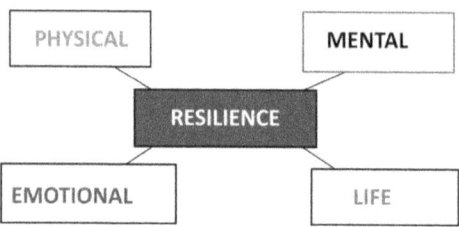

Build Physical Resilience

This is all about taking care of your body to boost your immune system so that you will be able to fight stress and stay healthy. Some of the most important things are:

- Eat healthy regular meals. Don't overeat or skip meals.
- Get physically fit. Do some regular exercise, it is 'active relaxation'.
- Take time out to relax. Make the time for 'passive relaxation'.
- Release tension and manage stress. Learn the strategies.
- Make sure you have plenty of sleep.

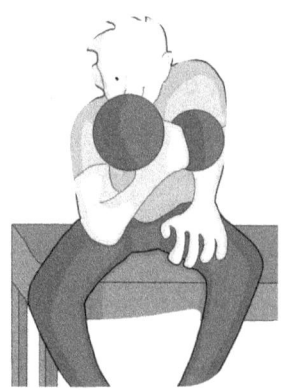

> *Obstacles don't have to stop you. If you run into a wall, don't turn around and give up. Figure out how to climb it, go through it, or work around it.*
>
> **Michael Jordan**

Balance Action Steps

Try this yoga pose for immediate stress relief:

- Breathe in and bring your arms above your head so your palms are facing each other.
- Bring your palms down until they are in front of your chest in the prayer position as you breathe out slowly.

Do this activity at least three times when you are feeling tense. It will relax you and help you better manage any stressful events that are occurring around you.

Build Emotional Resilience

This is all about managing your emotions and feelings. If you are experiencing a lot of the symptoms outlined in Chapter 5, Stage 2: **Stages and Effects of Stress**, then these are signals that you may not be coping. It is important to learn to manage your emotions. This will allow you to keep your body and your mind more balanced and grounded in difficult situations.

> *That which does not kill us makes us stronger.*
> **Friedrich Nietzsche**

A good question to ask yourself is — do you **REACT** or **RESPOND** to difficulties? If you tend to REACT, then you may experience many of the physical symptoms described in Stage 1: **Stages and Effects of Stress**, Chapter 5. If you RESPOND, you will generally be calmer and more balanced in the way you deal with things. Of course, the most difficult emotions to manage are the powerful ones, such as intense rage or extreme distress.

Immediate useful strategies include:

- Take several deep breaths.
- Count to ten.

- Take time out and come back to the discussion if your emotions rise.

Longer term strategies include:

- Reduce or reorganise your workload if possible.
- Gain support from people around you at work and home.
- On a personal basis, take up meditation, massage, or any other relaxing activities.
- Exercise, time out, or a holiday, will also help you build coping mechanisms so that you might stay calmer when powerful emotions arise.

Another important strategy to boost resilience is to be willing to receive support when you need it. Some people feel this is a sign of weakness but, in fact, it is actually an intelligent and brave thing to do. So ask for help and support when you are feeling very stressed or overwhelmed. Most people are quite happy to give support but are not so good at receiving it. Try it!

Balance Action Steps

Think of a recent time when you reacted negatively, and ask yourself the following questions:

1. **Why did I feel that way?** What caused my reaction? Was I actually over-reacting or was I justified in my feelings?
2. **What did I really want to happen?** What outcome did I really want from the situation?
3. **Whose problem was it really?** Was it mine or theirs? Was I reacting to something that just pushed my buttons, or did I genuinely have cause to feel that way?
4. **What assumptions was I making?** Was I making a 'mountain out of a molehill', or was I appropriate with my response?

Now think of how you could have responded differently to the situation. You will probably find that a calm and controlled approach might have avoided a lot of stress for all parties involved.

Build Mental Resilience

> *If you voluntarily quit in the face of adversity, you'll wonder about it for the rest of your life.*
>
> **Former US President Bill Clinton**

Put Things in Perspective

Put daily life crises in perspective. What's really important? How many of your fears and worries are actually real rather than imagined? Richard Carlson, author of *'Don't sweat the small stuff!'* says it is all small stuff.

Slow Down and Smell the Roses

Everyone seems to be so busy these days. People rush around and many claim they don't have enough hours in the day to get everything done. Few people in their last living hours would regret not working more, but many may regret not spending more time with loved ones or doing things they had always wanted to.

So why not pace yourself in your busy day. Taking an extra few seconds to do a task or to enquire after someone else can create the difference between being calm or tense. The calmer you are, the more in control you will feel.

Become Optimistic

Are you an optimist or a pessimist? Do you see the glass half full or half empty? Research from the US indicates that optimists will live 20% longer and be healthier during their lives. It also shows that optimism and resilience are better predictors of success at school than IQ.

Optimism is linked to wellbeing, morale and positive mood. It is also beneficial in coping with conflict, change and stress, perseverance and effective problem solving. Clearly it is good for both physical health and mental fitness to be optimistic. The good news is that you can learn to become so.

In his book *'Learned Optimism'* Martin Seligman, an eminent US psychologist and researcher defines optimism as having three aspects which are outlined below. He advises that we can all learn to become more optimistic by overcoming any pessimistic attitudes that apply to ourselves.

1. Optimists are more likely to see problems objectively whereas pessimists will tend to take similar things more personally.
2. Optimists generally see setbacks as temporary and 'bounce back' faster. Pessimists often see setbacks as permanent and can become resentful and angry.
3. Optimists are good at compartmentalising problems or disappointments. For example, they can mentally place them in a box and put it away, whereas pessimists let such problems or disappointments take over or pervade their lives.

The table below will help you better understand this theory.

ATTITUDE/ BELIEF	THE PESSIMIST	THE OPTIMIST
Personalisation	Blames self for outcome	Doesn't personalise outcome of event
Permanence	Sees event as permanent	Sees event as temporary
Pervasiveness	Allows event to affect whole of life	Compartmentalises event

Chapter 8 When the Going Gets Tough…

Case Study

Sue and Joan were both attracted to Bill, the new staff member who had recently started working at their company. They laughingly competed for his attention and both hoped he might ask them to the mid-year company dinner. Interestingly, he did not respond to either of them and instead asked Wendy the new sales executive to be his partner for the night.

Sue, being an optimist, did not take this to heart and paired up with another male employee with whom she was friendly to go with to the dinner. Joan, who tended to be a pessimist, took it very personally and felt most offended. She barely spoke to either Bill or Wendy for several weeks.

Sue was sure that there would be plenty of opportunities in the future to meet the man of her dreams and wasn't really fussed. Joan, however, was equally sure that there would not be another chance like this one that she had missed. After all she was over 30 years of age!

Sue felt a little disappointed when she saw how well Bill and Wendy were getting on at the dinner but she put it aside and enjoyed herself. After all she had plenty of positives in her life with great friends, a nice car, a good social life and a devoted pet dog. Joan decided not to go to the dinner and refused an invitation to go out with her girlfriends that night and later. She was grumpy at work and with her family and even stopped going to the gym as frequently. She developed a severe cold and had trouble shaking it off. She felt that generally life was unfair.

As you will note these are two completely different responses to the same event. The difference is in the attitudes of each of the women and the quality of their self-talk or their interpretation of the situation. Notice the different messages they gave to themselves. Clearly Sue spoke more positively to herself and took a 'bigger picture' view of events. Joan adopted a pessimistic 'victim mentality' about what had occurred. She did not see things in perspective but focused on a single event.

Which one of these two are you? Would you take the optimistic approach like Sue and be happier and more balanced in your responses or would you be more like Joan and feel victimised and unhappy at what has occurred? Remember it is all in the way you perceive events. Your choice!

Talk or think yourself up

Just as you can bring yourself down by gloomy and negative thinking, you can change your mood to be more optimistic by thinking more positively. While you can't stop the negative thoughts as they come automatically, you can acknowledge them, sit with them briefly if you wish, and then send them away, replacing them with more uplifting thoughts.

You can also elevate your mood using visualisation. For example, you can take yourself off to a quiet spot and think about a past pleasant experience such as a holiday or fun occasion. Let yourself re-experience the event in your mind just as it happened. You will find that you often feel better within yourself after doing this.

Balance Action Steps

Try switching a negative mood to a more positive one:

1. Settle yourself in a quiet spot and slow down your breathing.
2. Find a pleasant or happy memory and focus on that experience.
3. Let yourself become very absorbed in the memory and re-experience it just as it happened.
4. Enjoy what you enjoyed before, but in your mind this time.
5. Check your feelings afterwards. You may find that you are smiling and feel lighter and brighter that when you started.

Build Life Resilience

You can make your life more meaningful by creating your own happiness and wellbeing. Interestingly, research has shown that this will not come about by having more money or moving to a warmer climate. Neither will it come solely from staying healthy and being educated, although these things will definitely help.

Many people think having children will do the trick although some find their offspring a constant source of stress. Others say they have more pleasure from their pets, probably because they usually do as they are told and don't answer back.

Research by Martin Seligman indicates that wellbeing is enhanced by being an optimistic thinker, being fully engaged in life and work, having a partner or a strong social network, avoiding negative events and emotions, and finding meaning and purpose in life.

How do you create meaning and purpose in your life?

People experience a sense of purpose using skills or strengths to help others or by being part of something greater than themselves.

Be clear on your core values

What is really important to you? You may create a sense of meaning from doing things for others or perhaps you want to further educate yourself. Possibly you could do some volunteer work. Alternatively find a charity to donate to — maybe as a family or work group.

Support family, friends, colleagues and community

We know that social connections strengthen resilience, so become involved in community activities or develop group interests. For example, join the work social club or take up dance or art or craft classes or get involved in a group sporting activity.

Ensure Work-life Balance

Life balance is not so much a time issue as a values issue. Are you creating time for the things that really matter to you? Do you have enough time to spend with family and friends? Do you take time to enjoy hobbies, pets, travel, learning? Life is not a dress rehearsal, so make the time you need to do the things you really want before it is too late.

Balance Action Steps

Work on increasing meaning and purpose in your life. Write down the four resilience headings and under each one list one or two things that you believe are doable for you. Make sure you:

1. Clarify what is really important to you. What would make your heart sing?
2. Decide on some way to do something positive for yourself and others.
3. Work out how to build into your busy days some of the things you wish you could be doing but feel you don't have time for. You can always find creative ways to make time!

Chapter 8 When the Going Gets Tough...

Replay

- Practice self-care to build physical resilience.
- Work on managing your emotions better.
- Become mentally fit through developing perspective and optimism.
- Create meaning and purpose in life – try giving back.
- Ensure work/life balance.

Remember to pick one action from this chapter to include in the **Personal Action Planner** at the end of the book.

Chapter 9

Confidence is Cool

How to Develop Confidence and Manage Emotions

Dance Step: Break Dance

This style of dance calls for strength, skill, balance and acrobatic technique. It can be quite difficult to master and an important aspect of the dance is 'attitude'.

What Is Confidence?

Confidence is hard to describe as it is one of those intangible skills that we can either have or not have. People often find it difficult to build and maintain self-confidence. It is a little like motivation, as we know when we have it but find it hard to describe what it actually involves and how to get it.

Abilities, skills and intelligence are often not enough to be successful, as we need self confidence to get ahead. However, don't forget that even the most confident people have situations where they feel nervous, particularly in social or work situations. For example, walking into a party where you don't know many people, participating in a competitive sporting activity, making a speech, speaking out at meetings or giving important presentations.

Being unable to use or demonstrate confident behaviours can often disadvantage people. This can occur in job interviews, successful selling and marketing roles, exam conditions and in leadership positions, as well as social situations.

One approach to discover the nature of confidence is for you to examine how it feels and what it looks like. So think of a time when you felt really confident. How did it feel? Chances are you'll come up with descriptions like 'Positive', 'Calm', 'Influential', 'Valued', and 'In control'. Inner confidence is a feeling of self-assuredness and a belief in one's own skills and ability.

There is no doubt that confidence skills can be learned. If you practice regularly, you can build them slowly, increasing them with each successful experience you have. Very confident people are able to carry their confidence across many situations and, even if they actually feel nervous, they somehow manage to appear in control.

Where Does Confidence Come From?

Why are some people more confident than others? How do they manage it? Where does it come from? How do they maintain it?

If you ever spend time with a small child, you will gain confirmation that we are born confident. Small children believe they are the centre of the universe and good at everything. Often they feel invincible. However, as they grow older and reality sets in, confidence can wane in the face of different hurdles and barriers to achievements.

The amount to which we lose our confidence often depends on life events and interactions with people around us. In particular, family, friends, teachers and managers can either nurture or destroy our self-esteem through actions and words.

The good news is that, regardless of what has happened in the past, you can take positive steps to build your confidence and self-esteem.

Balance Action Steps

Think of a very confident person you know or work with. What do they do to create this impression? Write a list of their positive qualities and then, to the best of your ability, do what they do. If you know the person well, you can even ask them how they manage to seem so positive, upbeat or confident in their behaviour under high pressure or in difficult circumstances.

Becoming More Confident

To achieve a successful outcome in learning confidence skills, you need to do the following:

- Have a strong belief that you can build your confidence.
- Have the motivation to set goals and be willing to practice, practice, practice.
- Gain support from others to encourage you.
- Reward yourself for your efforts.

If you are someone who feels they lack confidence and you want to work hard on building it, you can motivate yourself through considering what might happen if you don't change. Take note that as there will initially be few rewards from the outside world, you need to reward yourself.

Consider what price you might be paying for a lack of confidence!

At work, for example:

- Perhaps you end up doing more than you would like because you can't say 'No'.

- You might watch others with less experience gain promotion.
- You see others take the credit for your ideas.
- You create the impression that you don't have an opinion of your own.
- You miss out on opportunities because you're frightened to take a risk.

And outside of work:

- Missing out on a great party because you didn't know many people going.
- Not presenting yourself at your best in a job interview.
- Saying 'No' to a friend who wants you to go on an overseas trip with them.
- Standing in a corner all night at an event when other friends were having a ball.

Try to 'fake it till you make it'. This is very simple to say, but not always easy to do. If you persevere and continue to practice this approach, you will find that it will actually become a habit and will slowly help you increase your confidence. The more you do it the more confident you will become and feel.

Three top tips to appear more confidence

1. Act and look confident

Remember that as you only have one opportunity to make a first impression, your presentation and grooming immediately impacts on people. So if you look smart, dress appropriately, and are well groomed, you are more likely to create an impression of being confident.

Body language and facial expression convey a very large part of meaning to others. They are critical for presenting a confident image, so maintain eye contact and smile at people to convey confidence. As well, stand tall, look up, keep your shoulders back and give a good firm handshake rather than the 'limp fish' handshake that many people find so off-putting.

2. Speak confidently

A few simple tips to appear more confident when talking to people include:

- Use strong positive language.
- Be assertive, not aggressive.
- Project your voice so that everyone in the group can hear.
- Don't overuse apologetic words such as 'I'm really sorry but…'.
- Work at influencing and selling your ideas.
- Practice in front of a mirror.

If you have difficulty in speaking out in groups or at meetings, try out the 'Five Minute Mouse Rule'. Within the first five minutes of any group gathering, you need to speak out loud. The fact that you have verbalised early in the piece will usually help you have the confidence to continue to do so throughout the event.

You can say something as simple as 'Would you like a glass of water?' or 'Would you like the air conditioning turned up?' Just actually hearing your own voice will help you speak out later.

3. Think confidently

If you keep in mind that your thoughts will affect your feelings and they will then affect your behaviour, it seems logical that you need to practice thinking positively and confidently. The little voice in our mind or our 'self-talk' is the key to thinking confidently.

As discussed in Chapter 4: **Throw Out Negative Thoughts** the majority of our self-talk is negative, so that when we are feeling vulnerable or down it can overwhelm us with negativity. Yet remember that the power to change self talk is yours. By using positive self-statements or affirmations, you can change your negative thinking which, over time, will improve your confidence and optimism.

> *Believe you can and you're half way there.*
> **Theodore Roosevelt**

Strategies for Building Confidence

Try Mental Rehearsal

This can be used to visualise a positive result or outcome of any action.

Try out in your imagination different ways of behaving in new or unfamiliar situations. This private mental rehearsal will help you feel more confident when in the actual situations. When you are in the real experience it will be more familiar to you and, through the mental rehearsal which you need to practice frequently, you will actually program your mind to feel more confident and positive in the situation itself.

Balance Action Steps

Think of something you need to do which is daunting at the moment. Find yourself a calm, quiet place and then rehearse the event in your mind exactly as you would like it to go.
Let it unfold in small incremental steps until you can imagine yourself behaving or speaking the way you want to. If you wish, you can add in a positive self statement or affirmation to enhance the experience. Keep reminding yourself of the good feeling of being in control and you are likely to find that your confidence will increase to the point where you feel like giving it a go.

Try Taking Some Risks

We usually avoid risks because of fear. This can be fear of the unknown, failure, rejection or even success itself. By not taking risks you are playing it safe in physical, financial and emotional terms. If you face the risk and work through it, you will discover that you are more able to overcome it now and in the future. You need to learn to confidently separate real risks from imaginary ones.

Balance Action Steps

Take a small risk in your current life. Think of something that you've been hesitating doing and give it a go. When you have faced the risk and worked through it, give yourself a small reward and possibly gain some support from others as you share with them your experience.

Remember that every time you take a risk you actually move out of your comfort zone which will then expand it. With repetition, you will gradually develop behaviours that will become more like habits and you will feel more confident about applying these.

> The biggest risk is not taking any risk... In a world that is changing really quickly, the only strategy that is guaranteed to fail is not taking any risks.
>
> **Mark Zuckerberg, Facebook Founder**

Apply These Confidence Strategies

Look for a Role Model

Find someone who is really confident and constantly watch what they do, how they speak, how they look and see if you can pick up any tips to overcome nerves or fear. If you know them ask for advice.

Maintain your self-belief by using positive self-talk

Acknowledge your fearful thoughts, sit with them briefly, and then send them away, replacing them with something that is more practical, productive and positive. Then make a commitment to some positive action and go out and practice the new behaviour.

Get a Coach or Mentor for support

This can be really helpful as you will have someone to discuss your fears with and seek advice from. The coach or mentor will encourage you to go out and try new approaches and new behaviours and will give you helpful advice should these not work, or give you reward and encouragement when they do.

> I think confidence is the most important thing. Not cockiness, but confidence.
>
> **Ellen Degeneres**

Work at Managing Your Emotions

Revisit this question from Chapter 8 on resilience and consider it honestly. Do you react or respond? In other words, when you feel confronted do you blurt out an emotional tirade which can worsen the situation or do you give yourself some time to think things through and then respond more calmly? Confident people are more likely to respond calmly.

When we react to a situation we are usually behaving impulsively and we can feel as though we've been forced to act in a certain way. Often we see someone or something else as the cause of our outburst. In contrast, when we respond, we behave thoughtfully in a way that leaves us feeling more in control.

When we lack confidence we are more likely to react and when we react we may feel overwhelmed, scared, outraged, hurt, agitated, frustrated, angry, sad, disappointed or anxious. As a result we may lash out verbally or physically, cry, blame others, withdraw or resort to tantrums.

This behaviour may sometimes offer short term rewards. For example getting angry may get you noticed, enable you to vent frustration or manipulate others. It may also increase your chances of getting your own way. Often this 'pay-off' can reinforce reacting rather than responding. In the long term though, constantly reacting is negative and may ultimately destroy relationships.

> *Negative emotions like hatred destroy our peace of mind.*
>
> **Matthieu Ricard, Buddhist Monk**

 **Replay**

- You have the power to create confidence.
- Fake it till you make it.
- Practice acting, speaking and thinking more confidently.
- Get a coach or mentor.
- Practice, practice, practice!
- Learn to respond not react.

Remember to pick one action from this chapter to include in the **Personal Action Planner** at the end of the book.

Chapter 10

Raise the Bar on Relationships

How to get on Better with Others

Dance Step: Irish Dance

Popularised through Irish Riverdance, this is a group dance and part of a broader social activity. It dazzles the imagination with expressive and vigorous movements.

Why are relationships often difficult?

Human relationships are the foundation of life so why do we often mess them up so badly? Relationships require give and take from both sides but both the give and the take must be equally balanced to ensure the best end result for all who are involved.

> *The quality of your life is the quality of your relationships.*
>
> **Anthony Robbins**

There has to be more than one person interacting to create a relationship, yet when conflict or differences arise, we frequently see ourselves as in the right and the others involved as being in the wrong.

Differences are inevitable in any relationship whether it be with a partner, family member, friend or colleague. We need to learn how to handle these differences so as not to create a negative or destructive outcome for those who are part of the interaction. Successfully negotiating such differences can enrich and build the relationship and empower the people who are involved.

It is often very important for some people to be 'right' in any difficult transaction. If this is you, then you need to take care that you don't take such a rigid stance that you become overly 'righteous'. Many of us don't take responsibility for our input into difficult situations and get into the 'blame game' against the other people involved so as to justify our own position.

Differences often arise because of a breakdown in communication. We all use varied communication styles. Some of these and their impact are shown below:

Improving personal relationships

Relationships at home and in the workplace can impact on each other positively or negatively. We generally go to work to earn money to support ourselves and our families and to learn new skills. Another vital part of being at work is the social interaction with other people. Good relationships create a sense of wellbeing, whereas if we don't relate well to our colleagues, this can negatively impact on our performance, our health and our behaviour at home.

People in supportive relationships at work or with friends, and in loving relationships with partners and family, are more likely to be healthier overall. They generally have stronger immune systems due to better emotional health. They seem to support each other practically and emotionally and usually feel happier and more content with life in general. This in turn helps to balance out any other problems occurring in their lives. As well, they are less likely to have mental or physical health problems and usually take better care of their general health.

A good tip is to stop verbalising your worries about them to someone who may have a problem. This will help them feel they are doing better and contribute to their overall wellbeing and immune strength. It can also help you to stop worrying about them as much.

Communicating in relationships to enhance wellbeing

Martin Seligman, who is also the American founder of the Positive Psychology movement, says that 'we are deeply social animals with an innate capacity for empathy. This enables us to have rewarding relationships with others'. He suggests that to improve communication in relationships we should make five positive statements for every negative statement we utter.

In his recent book 'Flourish' he recommends using 'active and constructive' responding to increase love and friendship and enhance wellbeing. He says that this can also decrease the probability of depression arising.

How does this work? Well, next time someone tells you something positive about their own life, try responding in a way that gets them to relive that positive moment with you. For example if a partner or friend tells you they have had a promotion you have several options in the way you respond. See the diagram below and the following examples of responses to understand this approach:

	Constructive	Destructive
Active	✓	X
Passive	X	X

An **Active/Constructive** response — 'Wow, that's great news! When did you hear it? How were you told? How did you feel about it?'

An **Active/Destructive** response — 'That's good, but you will probably get a salary increase and have to pay more tax.'

A **Passive/Constructive** response — 'Oh, that's great. What do you want for dinner?'

A **Passive/Destructive** response — 'Big deal, can you help me cook dinner?'

Balance Action steps

Think of the last time you reported some good news that was partially or completely overlooked by the person you were talking to. How did you feel?

What about the last time someone reported good news to you? How did you respond? How could you respond more actively and constructively if you heard that same news today?

Get over wounded pride

All too frequently people fall out, often over quite trivial issues, and then stop speaking and engaging with each other. Harsh words may be said which upset the other and both parties can suffer from wounded pride. This can happen both at work and outside work and often close friendships may end.

On many occasions one or both parties may wish to heal the rift but refrain from doing so because they feel that if they reach out they may:

- Look weak in the eyes of the world.
- Be seen to admit they were in the wrong.
- Be rejected by the other person.

If this has happened to you and you want to recover the friendship or good working relationship you may need to grow up, take a risk in approaching the other person and get over wounded pride.

Ironically, it is the person who makes the first move who is the most courageous because of course there is a chance that any advances may be rejected. However, breaking the silence is an indication of strength not weakness and is a mature and intelligent way to behave. Sometimes just making contact will be all that is needed for the relationship to return to its former closeness.

> *Sometimes you gotta shut up, swallow your pride*
> *and accept that you're wrong. It's not giving up.*
> *It's called growing up.*
>
> **Anonymous**

Case Study

Alan had come to see me for assistance to stop smoking. In the course of our conversation I asked him if he had good friends who would support him rather than encouraging him to continue. He somewhat wistfully told me about how he had fallen out with his best friend Phil when they had too much to drink at a buck's party and argued badly about something quite trivial. They both said hurtful words and as a result had not seen each other or spoken for almost a year.

Alan said he really missed Phil and heard about him from time to time as he was still friendly with Phil's brother. When asked as to why he had not attempted to heal the rift, he said that he did not want to look weak in front of his mates. We discussed this at length and I was able to suggest a different perspective about the person who made the first move being the stronger one. He did not seem convinced at the time.

Two weeks' later he returned for another stop smoking session and was bursting with his news. Apparently after our session he was arranging drinks for his birthday and when inviting Phil's brother, casually suggested that Phil might like to come and would be welcome. He was surprised that 10 minutes later he received a call from Phil who was overjoyed at the invitation. They met up later that week and he said it was as if nothing bad had occurred between them. He was amazed at how his simple suggestion had healed the rift.

Balance Action Steps

If there is someone in your life that you have fallen out with and you wish it were different, have the courage to contact them. If you believe that they might not respond positively, use a third party to pave the way. Try it and you might be pleasantly surprised. If you do nothing, then nothing good or different will happen.

Forgiveness is freeing

There will always be someone in your life that has hurt or upset you. One of the ways to move on from this is to forgive that person. Before you slam this book shut at the very prospect, be mindful of the fact that the act of forgiveness is not for them, but for you.

An enormous amount of energy is used up in hatred, anger and negativity towards the person whom you believe has wronged you. You may also be prone to mentally or verbally berating them or endlessly discussing what they have done to upset you. Not only is this exhausting and time consuming, but other people get heartily sick and tired of hearing about it, although many are too polite to say so but may start avoiding you as a consequence.

Forgiveness does not mean forgetting but just letting go. Forgiveness will set you free of the all consuming negative thoughts and anger. This in turn will improve your general wellbeing and help reduce any stress or anxiety that has occurred as a result.

> *The weak can never forgive. Forgiveness is the attribute of the strong.*
>
> **Mahatma Gandhi**

Don't waste time with jealousy

Jealousy is such a wasted emotion as it too can become all consuming. It takes up huge amounts of time and energy and causes terrible friction or frustration in any relationship whether it occurs at work or outside of the workplace.

In personal relationships it can result in separation or divorce and, at work or socially, can bring an end to friendships or former good working relationships. From any of these perspectives it can result in furious arguments, silence, sulking and avoidance. The person who is on the receiving end of jealousy will frequently become angry and annoyed and may not wish to engage with the jealous person. In the home this can be fatal for a relationship. At work one party may look for another job.

If the jealous person is your partner, a family member, a friend or colleague you know well, there are steps you can take.

Seven steps to beat jealousy

1. Make a joint agreement with a jealous partner about how you'll both behave regarding time apart and other people. If the jealousy is from a family member, friend or close colleague, tell them how they are making you feel and ask them to work on letting go the problems or issue. Make sure all parties are comfortable with any decisions reached and that they are willing to work with agreements reached.
2. Some people need a lot more reassurance than others which can be frustrating. If you don't mind constantly reassuring the person who is jealous, they will eventually feel more secure and won't need this so often.
3. Ask a jealous family member, friend or colleague to commit to making the relationship work better between

you and gently suggest they seek support if it is their own insecurity causing the jealousy.
4. Whenever you feel jealous, have the courage to admit your feelings to yourself and anyone else involved.
5. If you suffer from jealousy, work to improve your own attitude. Identify what unique qualities you bring to the relationship. Be mindful of your own positive attributes and why the relationship occurred in the first place.
6. Ask your partner to reassure you of his or her love and commitment to the relationship or a work colleague to maintain their commitment to improving the working relationship between you. If you suffer badly from jealousy, you may need to do this frequently, but be aware if the other person becomes irritated by this and back off.
7. If you and others continually create situations causing jealousy, consider finding a relationship counsellor to help you solve the problem. If it occurs with a colleague, you may need to undergo mediation with an external person who has experience in resolving personal or work-related conflict.

If all else fails

If you don't know the other person very well or are not able to implement these suggestions, then your only recourse might be to do your best to rise above the situation. Make an effort to take things professionally not personally. Keep reminding yourself that it is their problem not yours and stay away from them as much as possible.

Balance Action Steps

Think of someone in your life ...

- a) who has hurt you, or
- b) who is jealous of you, or
- c) of whom you are jealous.

What could you do differently to change the relationship?

How can you start to think about them differently?

Try changing any negative self-talk about them which can really make a difference to how you might respond. See Chapter 4: Throw Away Negative Thoughts to help with this.

> *Everything that irritates us about others can lead us to an understanding of ourselves.*
>
> **Carl Jung**

Replay

- Let go the need to always be 'right'.
- Create supportive relationships in and out of work.
- Use active and constructive communication.
- Get over wounded pride.
- Remember that forgiveness can set you free.
- Don't waste time with jealousy.

Remember to pick one action from this chapter to include in the **Personal Action Planner** at the end of the book.

Chapter 11

Coming Back from Setbacks

How to survive when things go wrong

Dance Step: Rumba

Originating from Cuba these sultry dance movements show emotions and the physical expressions of desire and forbidden love.

What causes setbacks?

The Macmillan Dictionary definition of a setback is:

> A problem that delays or that stops progress or makes a situation worse.

Life is full of ups and downs. There are always bumps in the road and we will often trip and fall. Sometimes this can be very painful. Life's survivors are those who pick themselves up, dust themselves off, attend to their wounds and keep moving on.

We generally think that we know what is best for us and what we want to achieve in life. Most of us believe that this will provide us with the happiness we so long for. It sounds good, but it is not usually the case! The reality of life is that all of us will encounter various setbacks at times.

Setbacks can include loss of a loved family member, friend, or pet, a physical injury, a relationship or friendship ending badly or suddenly, missing out on a promotion or a place on the team. They also include financial hardship, conflict with a family member or workmate, being made redundant, loss of a favourite or expensive possession, and many more.

From a mental health perspective if you suffer from the effects of depression, anxiety, anger or stress you are likely to have more downs than ups. How you learn to deal with the ups and downs of life will make a huge difference in successfully managing your problems or symptoms and coming out positively on the other side.

Everyone faces emotional upsets, disappointments and a sense of failure at times. If you can find a way to overcome your setbacks and keep going, you will get better, become stronger and feel happier for doing so. By persevering you will find you are more likely to reduce many of the symptoms of depression, anxiety, anger or stress.

What to do when you experience a setback

The trick is to learn how to deal with setbacks and develop the resilience to bounce back and even come out on top. The philosopher Friedrich Nietzsche famously said *'that which does not kill us makes us stronger'* and how true that is. All evidence shows that once you have successfully survived a setback you gain new strength and knowledge which will help you cope if something similar ever happens again.

It is extremely unlikely that you're going to face what life throws at you or successfully achieve your life goals and dreams without a few setbacks. Also keep in mind the times when your wishes didn't come true and it turned out to be a good thing for some reason.

When a setback occurs you have two choices. One is that you

can 'go under' by becoming emotionally distraught and feel trampled on by life. Be aware that this might result in you developing a victim mentality. The other choice is to take the attitude that a setback is only temporary, you can overcome it and better things will lie ahead. With the latter you are clearly much more likely to bounce or climb back.

Balance Action Steps

Stop and think about the last real setback you faced. How well did you manage it?

Write down a list of what helped you survive the setback.

Now write down a list of what you could do differently next time for a better outcome.

So how well do you deal with setbacks?

Try the quick quiz below.

For each statement, rate yourself from 1 to 5 where 1 = not often, 2 = occasionally, 3 = moderately well, 4 = quite often, 5 = most of the time; then total up your ratings.

- I stay calm in a crisis and usually take useful action. ___
- I can find humour in many tough situations and can laugh at myself. ___
- I ask lots of questions and want to know how things work. I am not afraid to make mistakes. ___
- I experiment and I like to try new ways of doing things. ___
- I constantly learn from experience so as to better manage the situation next time. ___
- I adapt quickly as I am very mentally and emotionally flexible. ___
- I can think in negative ways to reach positive outcomes e.g. I will ask 'What could go wrong, so it can be avoided?' ___

- I am comfortable with my contradictory personality qualities e.g. calm and emotional, gentle and strong. ____
- I have strong self-esteem and self-confidence. ____
- I expect to handle new situations well because of my past successes. I know my reliable strengths. ____
- I have good friendships and caring relationships. ____
- I am comfortable to express my feelings honestly. ____
- I am an optimist and expect most things to work out well. ____
- I have empathy for others and can usually see other perspectives. ____
- I frequently use my intuition and listen to my creative hunches. ____
- I stand up for myself and can find allies, resources, and support. ____
- I can turn misfortune into good luck and gain strength from adversity. ____
- When I experience a setback I usually ask 'How can I turn this around? Why is it good that this happened? ____
- I feel increasingly competent and resilient in my life. ____
- I enjoy life more and more as time progresses. ____

YOUR TOTAL SCORE ____

Dealing With Setbacks Quiz Score Key
- 80 or higher — you are great at dealing with setbacks!
- 65–80 — you do better than most
- 50–65 — you are moderately OK
- 40–50 — you're struggling
- 40 or under — you need help!

Top tips to push through setbacks

Look at the situation or event objectively
This can be difficult if you are highly emotional about what has happened. It is a good idea to talk it through with a trusted friend or work colleague who is not emotionally invested in what has occurred and listen to their thoughts or ideas. These are likely to be more practical and realistic than your emotionally charged response.

Decide whether the setback is a bad as it first seemed
If it is, seek professional help. However, sometimes anxiety can magnify the problem and it may be easier to overcome the setback than first thought.

Take responsibility where it is due
Don't become a martyr or victim and take it all on yourself if this is not appropriate. Simply acknowledge to yourself your part in what has happened.

Don't blame others
This can permanently end a relationship if the other person feels unfairly blamed or that you have not considered their side in the situation. Do your best to come to terms with what has occurred and then start planning what to do next. Facing things objectively will help with this. Look at what has worked for you in the past and if possible do something similar.

Ask for advice or assistance
Don't be too proud or embarrassed to ask for help. Some people think it is a weakness to do so whereas it is actually a brave and intelligent thing to do. Others feel bad about 'burdening' friends or family with their problems. Be aware that most people will want to help. How would you feel if the situation was reversed and a close friend or family member was in trouble and did not feel able to ask you for your support? Also others may have been in a similar situation and will have valuable advice to give you.

Don't beat yourself up about what has happened
Most of us don't deliberately create setbacks or unhappy or difficult situations. It is very hard to be perfect and unrealistic to try too hard to be so. Say no to perfect!

Don't live with regrets about the situation
Life is too short for regrets so be prepared to let the negatives go. Work out what is really important to you and head in that direction. Keep moving forward.

> *Life is not the way it's supposed to be. It's the way it is. The way you deal with it is what makes the difference.*
>
> Virginia Satir

Balance Action Steps

Go back to the setback you thought of previously.
Now write down a list of what you would do differently next time.

A Short Guide to Managing Setbacks

Stop and consider the situation objectively
Express your feelings to someone else
Take care not to catastrophise
Be willing to ask for help
Acknowledge your role without blaming yourself or others
Create plans for what to do next
Keep flexibly moving forward
Stay positive and motivated to find happiness

Decide Whether You Are a Quitter or a Fighter

Alexander Graham Bell, who is credited with inventing the first practical telephone, said '*When one door closes another door opens*'. While this may seem very clichéd if you are facing a difficult time, keep in mind that he also said '*but we so often look so long and so regretfully upon the closed door, that we do not see the ones which open for us*'.

There are always opportunities available and we just have to be flexible enough and willing to see them. If you are open to this belief you are far more likely to find something that will make you happy or show you the way to achieve your goals.

You need to choose whether to just give up or to persevere against any setbacks that occur in your life. If you decide to push through, you will have to face the setback, do something about it, get help if you need it and move on past it to the best of your ability.

You will need to gather your strengths, both physical and emotional and accept any help that you need. For helpful tips see Chapter 2: **Fortify Your Physical and Mental Fitness**. If necessary, seek professional help.

Balance Action Steps

Write down some steps you can take to deal with any current or recent setback. What can you do, who can help, how will you stay positive?

Now think about your strengths that will help survive the setback. What skills do you need to learn and what strengths do you need to develop more to help you succeed?

> *All the world is full of suffering. It is also full of overcoming.*
>
> **Helen Keller**

Replay

- We all experience setbacks and can either choose to push through them or succumb.
- Setbacks can be personal, emotional, physical or work related.
- Perseverance and a positive attitude will help you overcome setbacks.
- Face the setback, plan and take action, get help and move on.
- Be flexible, open and willing to see opportunities that exist.
- Keep moving forward without regrets. Look for happiness.

Remember to pick one action from this chapter to include in the **Personal Action Planner** at the end of the book.

Chapter 12

Seize the Day!

How to live life to the full

Dance Step: Jazz

Jazz is a fun dance that relies heavily on originality and improvisation. Dancers mix different styles incorporating their own expression. Love, life, despair, tragedy, hope, compassion, nostalgia and optimism are all part of jazz.

Create the life you want

Life is rarely the way we expect or want it to be, life is just the way it is. Life is what happens while we are watching it pass us by. We watch it unfold before us and then eventually we leave it. While we may not have much control over our birth and our death (other than by keeping as fit and healthy as we can to prolong our lives) we certainly can influence the journey as it moves from start to finish.

In western society we are able to create a life where we can be happy or sad, miserable or joyous. We can be active or passive, a 'go-getter' or a watcher. We can dance in the direction of our dreams, but when we stumble, many of us complain about how we never get what we want.

We can experience the delicious taste of success or the bitterness of failure. Some of us die regretting what we haven't done rather than with the satisfaction of having at least 'given it a go', even if we haven't succeeded.

When we are young life seems infinite, but as we grow older it soon starts to feel shorter and we start wondering how we will fit in all the things we want to do. Don't waste precious time. Write out your 'Bucket List' (as in the movie of the same name starring Jack Nicholson and Morgan Freeman) and get started doing the things that you want to do before you leave this earthly realm.

Remember, it is not the years you live that are important but the quality of the life you live. Live every day as if it is your last, because you never know what tomorrow may bring.

> *There are only two ways to live your life. One is as though nothing is a miracle. The other is as though everything is a miracle.*
> **Albert Einstein**

Keep things in perspective

We often focus negatively on events or situations that seem like a big deal but in reality may be quite insignificant in the grand scheme of things. So, you need to put the daily negative events that occur in life and work — the ones that may seem to you like crises — in perspective and get clear on what's really important.

Rarely is everything occurring in life a disaster, but we often allow one or more problems to overwhelm the things that are actually working well for us. In difficult times we can tend to see the whole of life as a problem rather than identify just those particular aspects which are problematic. For example, you might have a couple of bad days and then tell others 'this has been a terrible week' when the other days in the week may have been perfectly fine.

When we magnify what has occurred due to emotions winning over judgment, we run the risk of exaggerating things out of proportion. So we first need to carefully consider the true importance of a situation and look at it calmly before deciding what to do next. Hopefully, we can then stop ourselves from over-reacting and potentially creating a problem for ourselves and others or, alternatively, making things worse.

Let go of what doesn't really matter

Be aware that any situation can be perceived as either a catastrophe or a challenge, it is simply a matter of how we view it. As mentioned previously, Richard Carlson author of 'Don't sweat the small stuff!' says it is *all* small stuff, yet we frequently let small problems in life create an upset. He advises us to live in the now, let others strive for fame and fortune, do one thing at a time and learn to lower our stress tolerance (see Chapter 5 for tips).

> *Do not anticipate trouble or worry about what may never happen. Keep in the sunlight.*
> **Benjamin Franklin**

Action Steps for Better Balance

Look at an example of 'The Big Picture' below:

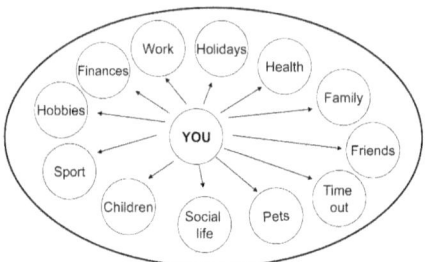

Each circle represents some of the common factors in people's lives. Decide which ones are currently working for you and those that are not okay.

In the table below tick those that are working and cross those that are not. You may need to add some in or change some for relevance to yourself and your own life.

Work		Social life	
Health		Children	
Family		Sport/Exercise	
Friends		Hobbies	
Time out		Finances	
Pets		Holidays	

You are most likely to find some things in your life which are working well and in balance. Allow yourself to experience the satisfaction of those.

Now it's time to address things that are not working. Make a list of them and add some positive actions you can take. If necessary get some help but don't just leave things as they are. Remember, if things are not working for you, then don't keep doing more of the same. Try something different. It might actually work!

Have a go at happiness

Most people will say they want to be happy. So what does it mean to achieve happiness? Happiness means many different things to different people. To some, it is living a good life, having a loving relationship or lots of friends. To others it may be a prestigious job, or owning their own home, or being financially secure.

Wikipedia defines happiness as:

> *A mental state of well-being characterized by positive or pleasant emotions ranging from contentment to intense joy.*

There are those who have little and yet are very happy, while others who have what appears to be a great deal can be unhappy and miserable. How happy you are seems to be determined by how you see yourself and your world and how you fit into that world. Happy people are usually in love with life and are able to grow and flourish throughout their lives.

What actually makes us happy?

Public surveys have found that partnerships and pets can make us happy, whereas surprisingly children don't always do so. Money will not create happiness, but freedom and a positive attitude does. Interestingly, youth and old age appear to be the happiest times. Studies have found that the happiest people spend the least time alone and the most time socialising. They seem to manage bad events better and they tend to 'bounce back' faster. They are frequently healthier, live longer and are more productive and successful over time.

Dr Martin Seligman, mentioned in previous chapters, is the founder of the Positive Psychology movement in the US which began in 1997. As a leading writer on optimism and wellbeing, he urged the profession of psychology to foster building human strengths rather than working so hard at trying to overcome their weaknesses. He believes that this will help counteract the world wide increase in depression and create more lasting happiness for individuals.

Studies on identical twins have concluded that around 50% of a person's self reported happiness can be inherited. Further studies have indicated that life circumstances influence around 10% of potential happiness, which then leaves approximately 40% of happiness under our own control.

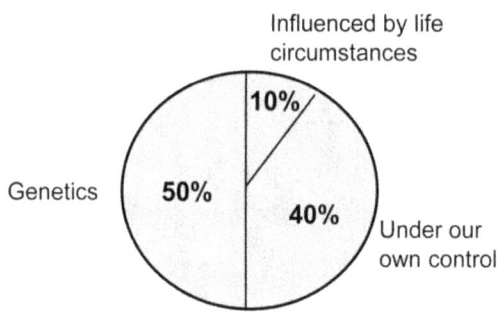

Determinants of Happiness

Positive psychologists believe that you can train yourself to be happier. They are developing strategies to counteract the tendencies many of us have to focus on the negative aspects of our lives. These work by boosting positive emotions about the past, by teaching us to enjoy the present moment and acknowledge our achievements. They also encourage us to develop positive relationships and to increase the amount of involvement and meaning we have in our lives.

The happiest, healthiest, most successful people in this world of ours are all doing something they love, creating something they believe in and living a life full of purpose and passion.

> *Each of us can be as happy as we choose to be.*
> Abraham Lincoln

So how can you become happier?

Do what gives you pleasure

Pleasure is a positive emotion and you can work on increasing it. Take the time to look at your life and, within reason and whenever possible, choose to do what gives you pleasure. In addition to doing what is important to you and what has to be done, you can also make feeling good a high priority when choosing from life's options.

But be aware that pleasure is usually temporary and may only last for a short period of time. For example, there is evidence that within a year of the event that changed their lives, both lottery winners and paraplegics generally revert to their former levels of either good cheer or sadness and melancholy.

Become really involved in life

Become a real part of something. This may involve your work or family or your friends. It may be involvement in a social or sporting club, or an art, dance or music group, or you might take more part in your local church or community. Create new friendships and activities to enjoy and have fun with. This will be more lasting and provide greater satisfaction and enjoyment than mere pleasure alone.

Create meaning and purpose in what you do

This requires going beyond self-interest for the good of others. You may choose to do some volunteer work, donate to a good cause or help out an elderly neighbour. If you can serve someone or some purpose that you believe is greater than you are, then this provides the greatest satisfaction and happiness of all.

Find your passion

Your passion is what gets you motivated to get out of bed in the morning. It puts a smile on your face and a spring in your step. You feel creative, excited and energised and have a sense of doing what is right for you. You know you have been living or working to your passion during those times when you feel most alive.

> *Passion is energy. Feel the power that comes from focusing on what excites you.*
>
> **Oprah Winfrey**

Balance Action Steps

1. Make a pleasure list

Write down list of the people, places, and activities that make you feel more positive and put a smile on your face or song in your heart when you think about them or do them. Then make an effort to see those people or places or do those activities.

2. Make a 'life involvement' list

Write down list of family or social activities that you would enjoy and that you can organise. Decide what you can do to become more happily involved in your work or with your colleagues. Write down some group activities that you can pursue, for example join a sporting or book club, a painting or craft group.

3. Make a 'meaningful life' list

Write down a list of things you can do to 'give back'. Is there someone you know that needs help or is there a charity you have thought about getting involved in. Is there someone in your life that has helped you in the past that you have always meant to thank? Is there some small thing you can do that will make a positive difference to someone else? These things create meaning in life.

4. Make a passion list

List your top five passions. Now work out how you can incorporate them into your day to day life or work. Think about what steps you can take, where you might go and who might help you to include these in your life away from work. Next clarify what work areas might include these passions. Now consider how you could possibly get into such work and what role you could take.

Turn Lemons into Lemonade

Dale Carnegie, the author of How to Win Friends and Influence People, famously said 'When fate hands you a lemon, make lemonade'. Take heed of this extremely good advice and find something in your life that you can change to be more positive. Look for things that help you feel better in the moment. This may come from giving or receiving affection, from people, nature, art, music, literature or from someone else's good deeds. When you find something, or create something that gives meaning to your life, hold on to it tightly so you will remember it should you need it again.

Victor Frankl was a holocaust survivor and eminent psychotherapist who died in 1997. After the Second World War he was released from a concentration camp having endured three years of dreadful and unimaginable suffering. He later wrote a book entitled *Man's Search for Meaning* in order to show that life has meaning under any circumstances. He writes of the beauty of the setting sun and its moving effect on the prisoners, something which the guards could not take away. Frankl believes the reason for his survival was the inner strength he derived from finding meaning in life even under such dire circumstances.

Balance Action Steps

Try this **'Three Good Things'** exercise.

At the end of each day for a whole week, write down three things that went well that day and say why. They can be quite simple such as 'I had a phone call from an old friend and it was great to catch up' or, 'I went for a walk in the park and enjoyed being in nature'. Don't be surprised if you find yourself looking at the world with a new perspective. You may find yourself feeling more positive or even start to feel happier at times. This is a proven happiness or well being booster for many people. If it works for you, then keep it up!

> *We are all in the gutter, but some of us are looking at the stars.*
>
> **Oscar Wilde**

Chapter 12 Seize the Day!

Replay

- Life does not always turn out the way we want it to.
- Don't waste time grumbling, get on and do the things you want to do before you die.
- Keep things in perspective. Look at the 'big picture.'
- Find out what makes you feel happy and go for it.
- Turn lemons into lemonade.
- You can learn to be happier so give happiness a go.

Remember to pick one action from this chapter to include in the **Personal Action Planner** at the end of the book.

Chapter 13

Dance towards Your Dreams

How to create the life you want

Dance Step: The Salsa

This dance is playful and fun and is a creative and unique form of self-expression representative of the dancer's personality and sensuality.

Make your dreams a possibility

We all have dreams, hopes and wishes but many of us dismiss them as being impossible to fulfill. Keep in mind that you first need to have the vision in order to turn it into a reality. In other words, you need to have some idea in which direction to head or what actions to take so as to get there.

Of course not all dreams will come true, but it is amazing how many actually will manifest in some way. Importantly, you also need to have the right mindset to forge ahead toward a particular vision or goal, as well as the confidence that you will reach it. To realise a dream you first have to sign up to the attempt, but take care that you don't lose what is real because you are too focused on the fantasy.

We know that goals are more readily achieved when they are written down and also when they are shared with others. You need to decide what it is you really want from life, making sure it is your own dream, not someone else's. Then you can write it down as your true heart's desire. Don't confuse yourself at this stage with worrying how you will get there.

You will actually begin to feel more confident about achieving a dream when you tell other people as it will start to seem more 'real' to you. Also, when you share it with others, you may be pleasantly surprised at how supportive they are. They may even come up with some good ideas as to how to proceed.

Mix with people who will uplift and motivate you and help you believe your dreams are possible. If you do this, another positive outcome is that you may create unexpected opportunities to help you get closer to your dream.

> *Go confidently in the direction of your dreams.*
> *Live the life you have imagined.*
> **Henry David Thoreau**

Believe in your dreams

Of course you need to believe that your dreams are possible. A positive attitude goes a long way in helping you reach your goal. In simple terms you need to know what you want to happen so that you can make it happen.

Use visualisation techniques

This is a helpful strategy to make the vision more real. You can imagine yourself having successfully achieved your dream or goal and experience how you want to feel and what you want to happen. Evidence has shown that when we imagine we are doing something, the changes that occur in our brain are the same as when we actually take that action.

Write down a positive self-statement

A self-affirmation about achieving your dream is another technique for feeling more confident and optimistic about your potential for success. The more you focus on what you want, the more likely you are to create it. This helps create a more positive mindset.

There is nothing magical about this but the concept was regularly dismissed by the scientific community. Interestingly, there has been a recent advent of a new science called neuroplasticity as described by Dr Norman Doidge in his international best seller *The Brain that Changes Itself*. Through his work we now know that the brain is not a rigid, machine like structure with brain cells continually breaking down with age and injury, but rather it is malleable and can change and develop.

There is now evidence to show that if we continually focus on a new thought or action and continue to increase this focus regularly, we can create new neural pathways in the brain and make positive and lasting changes.

> **Balance Action Steps**
>
> As it is beneficial for making your dreams happen to practice these techniques, why not give them a go? Think of something you would like to happen in your life. When you are in a relaxed and quiet mode, create a picture in your mind of a particular goal or dream and focus on successfully achieving what you want. At the same time say a positive self-statement related to creating this outcome. Some examples are:

- I will successfully finish my studies (visualise graduating).
- I will travel overseas (picture yourself in a desired overseas destination).
- I will have a successful career (see yourself in a hoped for occupation).
- I will find the right partner (imagine yourself with the person you want to be with).

The more you do this the more likely you are to make the dream happen. As you become better at this technique you can expand the breadth and depth of your goals and dreams. Just keep at it and remember that positive thinking can help create positive outcomes!

Tips to help you in the dance towards your dreams

Take the first steps

Write down your dreams and share them with other people.

Keep a confident mindset

Stay confident that you are on the right path and don't let setbacks become permanent obstacles.

Find others who are living your dream

Read about them, write to them, talk to them, model on them. Ask for advice and tips.

Practice aspects of your dream

If you have the opportunity to take some action relevant to your dream then do it. For example, if you want to be a successful dancer, artist or writer, enroll in a dance, painting or writing class.

Stay positive and hopeful that you will achieve your dream

Keep a positive attitude that you will achieve your dream. Mix with people who will support you and encourage your journey.

Use visualisation and affirmations

Frequently create a mental image of achieving your dream and write down a positive self-statement to support it. Repeat the statement to yourself when seeing the mental picture. Practice it regularly.

Let the sun rise on your dreams

Achieving a dream is a wonderful event and is like the dawn of a new day. Life is short and precious so don't waste it. Live your life to the fullest possible for you, so that some of your dreams may actually have a chance to come true.

Balance Action Steps

1. Think carefully and deeply what it is you really want from life.
2. In a clear and simple statement write down one of your dreams.
3. Decide on whom you will share this with and do so honestly.
4. Take on board any good suggestions offered.
5. If necessary ask others for advice on how to get to where you want to go.
6. Say a resounding 'yes' to any offers of help or opportunities that will take you closer to your dream.

Take an Optimistic Approach to Life

As discussed in Chapter 8: **When the Going Gets Tough**… optimists live longer and are happier and healthier in life. They also cope better with change, uncertainty, conflict and stress.

Optimists accept life as it is and don't constantly wish for it to be better. They see challenges as opportunities. They appreciate what they have, without whining about what they don't have. They are easier and more uplifting to be around as they don't bring others down with pessimism and negativity.

Think carefully about yourself and how you behave around others. Are you an optimist or pessimist? If you think you tend toward pessimism, then work on changing your self talk and become more optimistic which will benefit you, your health, your family, friends and co-workers.

Use the Power of Hope

The Oxford Dictionary describes hope as:

> *A feeling of expectation and desire for a certain thing to happen.*

The power of hope is its motivating force. Hope will keep us persevering towards something we want and moving forward. It can also be an agent of change. If the change is beneficial then this leads to more hope for creating the life we want.

People with higher levels of hope have been shown to be generally healthier, more effective at problem solving and more adjusted psychologically. A sense of hope will help you make better decisions about your goals. While hope is a great motivator, at the same time you need to ensure that your expectations and hopes are realistic so as to avoid disappointments and let downs.

Strategies to stay hopeful

Focus on success rather than failure

Keep reminding yourself of the times when things you have hoped for have come to fruition.

Learn to enjoy the challenge

Enjoy the process of actually getting to your goals. Don't focus only on the final attainment.

Have a positive emotional state when thinking about what's next

Make sure you are feeling upbeat when planning or thinking ahead. This will keep you keen and motivated.

Consider alternative pathways when the original direction is changing

Look for other ways to get to where you want to go if obstacles arise. Seek advice or support to overcome roadblocks.

Don't distract yourself with self-defeating thoughts

Stay focused and on task. If you have any negative or self-defeating thoughts, acknowledge them and let them go. Replace them with a positive take on your hopes and goals. See Chapter 5: **Throwing Away Negative Thoughts,** to help with this.

Action Steps for Better Balance

Find a 'hope buddy'

Depending on what you are currently wishing for, share your hopes with a good friend or work colleague. Talk openly about your goals for the future and brainstorm ways of getting there.

Write a hope story

Write down what you hope for and re-read it over and over to reinforce your efforts. If you feel comfortable to do so read it to your friends and family.

Practical Strategies to Make Your Dreams a Reality

Map your current status

Create a map of where you are financially, physically, socially and with your career. Ask yourself:

- What are your strengths?
- What do you need to change most?
- What do you need to start doing?
- What do you need to stop doing?
- What information do you need?
- Who can you ask for this information?

Chunk Down Your Approach

Break down your path towards your overall goal or dream into small manageable and achievable steps so the overall journey seems less daunting. As you achieve each smaller goal give yourself a small reward to maintain motivation.

Schedule Your Smaller Goals

Use a diary or calendar to regulate your small steps so they become a habit. Thus might include savings, exercise, or classes for example.

Identify Potential Blockers

Be aware of what might get in the way and find strategies to overcome these barriers. These might include time constraints, money owed, lack of motivation, lack of confidence from family or friends that you will succeed. Ask for help and advice if necessary to get over these hurdles. Consider getting a life coach.

Be Flexible if Your Dream Changes

You are only human, so dreams and priorities can change with changing circumstances. No problem if this happens. Just move the goal posts until you are heading in the direction you want.

Find the right People to Support You

Oprah Winfrey recommends surrounding yourself with only people who will lift you higher. Such people will support and encourage you to realise your dreams. Don't be put off by the 'nay sayers'. It's your dream. Go for it!

Balance Action Steps

To get started close your eyes and visualise what it would be like if you had achieved your dream.

- Where would you be?
- What would you be doing?
- Who else would be there?
- How would you be feeling?

Record your responses to check on your progress along the way.

The future belongs to those who believe in the beauty of their dreams.

Eleanor Roosevelt

 **Replay**

- Believe in your dreams.
- Write them down and share them with others.
- Practice techniques to make your dreams happen.
- Become an optimistic glass half full person and live longer.
- Use the power of hope to help achieve your goals and dreams.
- Use practical strategies to make your dreams reality.

Remember to pick one action from this chapter to include in the **Personal Action Planner** on the next page.

Learn to Dance on a Moving Carpet
Personal Action Planner

Chapters	Favourite tip	Who will help?	By when
1. Self Awareness: The Key to a Better Life How to know yourself better			
2. Fortify Your Physical and Mental Fitness How to keep your mind and body strong and healthy			
3. Sleep Soundly How to get a good night's sleep			
4. Throw Away Negative Thoughts How to think more positively			
5. Stay Stress Savvy How to better manage life's stressors			
6. Become Fearless How to cope with anxiety			
7. Rise Above the Dark Clouds How to survive despite depression			
8. When the Going Gets Tough…. How to build resilience to beat stress			
9. Confidence is Cool How to develop confidence and manage emotions			
10. Raise the Bar on Relationships How to get on better with people in life and work			
11. Come Back from Setbacks How to survive when things go wrong			
12. Seize the Day! How to live life to the full			
13. Dance towards Your Dreams How to create the life you want			

Don't forget to celebrate or reward yourself as you achieve each goal!

Bibliography

Richard Carlson: *Don't sweat the small stuff!*

Dale Carnegie: *How to Win Friends and Influence People*

Jacky Dakin & Kathryn McEwen: *Short Poppies can Grow: Confidence at Work* (Currently available from Halifax House Consulting, 206 Halifax Street, Adelaide or via www.shortpoppiescangrow.com/shortpoppies/)

Dr Norman Doidge: *The Brain That Changes Itself: Stories of Personal Triumph from the Frontiers of Brain Science*

Sarah Edelmen: *You Can Change Your Thinking*

Victor Frankl: *Man's Search for Meaning*

Louise Hay: *You Can Heal Your Life* (This New York Times Bestseller has sold over 30 million copies worldwide)

David Lykken and Auke Tallegen: *Happiness is a Stochastic Phenomenon* (University of Minnesota)

David T. Lykken: *The Heritability of Happiness* (University of Minnesota)

Sonja Lyubomirsky: *The How of Happiness*

Martin Seligman: *Learned Optimism*

Martin Seligman: *Flourish: A New Understanding of Happiness and Well-Being — and How to Achieve Them*

Michael D. Yapko: *Treating Depression with Antidepressants: Drug-Placebo Efficacy Debates Limit Broader Considerations.* (American Journal of Clinical Hypnosis, 2013)

Michael D. Yapko: *Depression is Contagious*

Michael D. Yapko: *Breaking the Patterns of Depression*

www.ingramcontent.com/pod-product-compliance
Lightning Source LLC
Chambersburg PA
CBHW051751230426
43670CB00012B/2245